The
Channel Four Racing
Guide to
RACECOURSES

CHANNEL FOUR RACING GUIDES

edited by Sean Magee

already published

FORM AND BETTING

with Jim McGrath and John McCririck

The Channel Four Racing Guide to RACECOURSES

with
DEREK THOMPSON
and members of the Channel Four Racing team

edited by
SEAN MAGEE

MACMILLAN

First published in 1998 by Channel 4 Books, an imprint of Macmillan
Publishers Ltd, 25 Eccleston Place, London SW1W 9NF and Basingstoke

Associated companies throughout the world.

ISBN 0 7522 2198 1

Text © Sean Magee and contributors 1998
Photographs © George Selwyn 1998
Line drawings © Racing Post 1998

The right of Sean Magee to be identified as the author of this
work has been asserted by him in accordance with the
Copyright, Designs and Patents Act 1988.

9 8 7 6 5 4 3 2 1

A CIP catalogue record for this book is available from the British Library.

Commissioning Editor: Susanna Wadeson
Editors: Mari Roberts and Gillian Bromley
Design and production by Production Line
Printed by Mackays of Chatham plc, Chatham, Kent

This book accompanies the television series Channel Four Racing
made by Highflyer Productions for Channel 4.
Executive producers: John Fairley and Andrew Franklin

Contents

Illustrations

All photographs in the colour section between pages 64 and 65 are by George Selwyn.

The course plans are reproduced by kind permission of the *Racing Post*.

The map on page 28 is by Jackie Hunt.

Preface

The aim of the *Channel Four Racing Guides* is to provide enthusiasts with basic information about different aspects of horse racing which will enhance their enjoyment of the sport, be it in the betting shop, on the racecourse, or watching on television. It is – as Tommo is wont to say – as simple as that.

That the variety of Britain's racecourses forms an enduring and endearing element of the sport's appeal has come to be one of racing's most frequently uttered clichés; but it is also incontrovertibly true, as anyone who has gone racing at, or seen on television, even a handful of the tracks described in this book will recognise. Different shapes and sizes, different standards of sport, different levels of facility, different atmospheres – Britain's courses provide an exhilarating spectrum of racing experiences, and if this book encourages you to sample for the first time some of those moods, or to renew your acquaintance with Cartmel or Newmarket or Market Rasen, it has served its purpose.

As this book goes to press, early in August 1998, change is in the air. Lingfield Park and Windsor have both announced that they are to drop jump racing: Windsor at the end of 1998, Lingfield in March 1999. But you lose some, you win some, and moves have been made to add to the map of British racecourses with a completely new track. In 1997 an application to build a new course at Pembrey in South Wales was turned down by the British Horseracing Board, but undaunted investors are reputedly beating a path to the BHB's door with plans for new courses in the south-east at such places as Thurrock in Essex and Fairlop in East London. It could be that the next edition of this book will be significantly different. We shall see.

Meanwhile, thanks as usual to Andrew Franklin and all the Channel Four Racing team, especially to the presenters; and a particular mention for John McCririck, who took the news that he could not have Alexandra Park as his favourite racecourse with a touching equanimity. Thanks also to Susanna Wadeson at Macmillan (come back – all is forgiven); Sandy Holton at Channel Four; Robert Cooper, Phillip Jones and Andrew Parker for all sorts of help; Mari Roberts for her inhuman serenity during the production process; George Selwyn for the photographs; and Gillian Bromley and Charlie Webster for the customary miracles.

Sean Magee

Come racing!

Derek Thompson

Racecourses have been places of magic for me since my first ever day's racing – at Stockton-on-Tees at the ripe old age of eight. The course at Stockton, later renamed Teesside Park, has long since gone, but the memory of that first close encounter with a racecourse has never faded. I also remember that it only cost four shillings – twenty pence at today's prices – to have a bet on the Tote!

Another local track in my childhood was Sedgefield, and on one very early outing there my father had sat my brother Howard and myself right on the running rail just after the winning post. But my mother demanded that we moved, as she said it could be dangerous being so close to the action – and sure enough, just two minutes later a horse got loose and crashed into the rail at the very point where Howard and I had been trying to get the best vantage point. But for my mother's insistence that day, I might not be here writing this . . .

Stockton-on-Tees and Sedgefield were the main courses of my childhood, but it was at another of the north-east tracks, Redcar, that I had an early brush with televised racing: the late, great John Rickman, doyen of ITV racing presenters, went round some of the younger members of the crowd asking what they wanted to be when they grew up, and D. Thompson said he wanted to be a racing correspondent on television. If only I was that clairvoyant every time I give my Charity Bet on *The Morning Line*! Some time after that brief encounter I was regularly back at the course presenting a racing programme for Radio Teesside, and I still love returning there with Channel Four Racing.

My early years also took me to Kelso, that beautiful track in the Border Country. My father, who had a few point-to-pointers and hunter-chasers, sent a horse to Kelso with what we thought was a good chance. Howard – who was to ride it – and I went up with the horse and found ourselves staying in the Temperance Hotel, which unfortunately lived up to its name. In the race Howard fell at the first fence and the horse's bridle came off, which meant we had to spend hours rounding up our charge. Despite that early experience, I still love a day at Kelso (though I no longer stay at the Temperance Hotel).

In fact, even after all these years of being professionally involved with the sport I can honestly say that I still look forward to every single day's racing, whether with Channel Four Racing, or as a course commentator, or just one of those rare days out with no working commitments. Every course has a separate character, and to me they're like fifty-nine different friends – some very relaxed, others rather more formal, but each with its own foibles.

And each has its own characteristic sound, its individual background noise of local voices. I love encountering different dialects and accents – from 'och ayes' up at Ayr to rural 'ooh-aahs' down at Exeter, with the Cockney you can hear at Sandown or Epsom, the Welsh at Chepstow and Bangor and the Geordie lilt at Hexham and Newcastle all giving the on-course experience its special flavour.

It's not only British accents, either. What would Cheltenham in Festival week be without the Irish brogue you hear at every turn? And plenty of visitors from further afield are drawn to the British racing scene by the sheer variety of our racetracks: in July 1998, for instance, I interviewed an American visitor, Sue Edwards, who was so captivated by British courses that she had visited all fifty-nine over the past two years!

In my time I've visited most of Britain's courses in a working capacity, and I've been privileged to get first-hand experience of many of them not only as commentator or television presenter, but as a rider too. In my days as an amateur jockey I rode over many of the jumps tracks, and Plumpton will always have a very special place in my affections: it was here in March 1980 that I scored my one and only win under Rules, in a charity race over two miles on the flat. This was one of the great moments of my life, but might have attracted less notice from the media at large had not the runner-up been ridden by one HRH The Prince of Wales. Prince Charles was riding the 7–4 favourite Long Wharf, but I took up the running on Classified a furlong out and we held on by two lengths. I'd borrowed a pair of trainer Nicky Henderson's breeches for the race, and I must be a bigger lad than Nicky because in the closing stages of the race they split along the flies – causing one paper to bill me as 'The Outsider Who Flashed Past The Prince'. I love it!

Classified himself was a four-year-old then, and after the race I expressed interest in buying him. But Nicky put me off, suggesting the horse had limited potential – which was unfortunate advice, because by the time Classified retired he had won twelve races over fences and run third in West Tip's Grand National. His performance at Plumpton might not have been absolutely his finest hour, but it was certainly mine, and it puts the Sussex track right up there with my favourite courses.

A bit lower down in my hit parade of racecourses is Catterick, which can be a real bugger of a place when you're riding a novice chaser. I was run away with here once on the way to the start for a two-mile chase, and just about managed to get control by the time the race was off. But they go a million miles an hour over two miles at Catterick and my horse and I had a disagreement just before the first fence. I saw a stride, he didn't, and the result was a crashing fall. Riding in a novice chase at Catterick is not an experience I'd recommend.

The jewel in Channel Four's crown, at least as far as jumping is concerned, is the National Hunt Festival at Cheltenham, another of those courses which has meant so much to me over the years. Although I never rode there – I think a place like that is best left to the pros! – I did lead up a couple at Cheltenham (though not at the Festival) when I was looking after my father's horses, and as a racegoer saw many of the greats run there.

I'm often asked which is my favourite track, and I'd have to put Newmarket and York as my joint number ones. The quality of racing at both is just outstanding. In terms of quality, Ascot is obviously in the same league, and the Royal Meeting in June one of the great highlights of the year. Since Ascot is firmly in the BBC's grasp I can, other commitments allowing, concentrate on enjoying four days of the best racing in the world, and the wonderful pageantry of the Royal Procession before each day's programme gets under way.

Yet I also love racing at the other end of the quality spectrum, at the jumping 'gaffs' with their strong local feel and cosy atmosphere. And I really enjoy the all-weather tracks, especially when a good meal is in prospect: the food at Southwell is superb, as it is in the panoramic restaurant at Wolverhampton.

The variety which is the essence of the British racing scene is reflected in the range of courses we cover at Channel Four – from great occasions like Derby Day, the Cheltenham Festival or the York August Meeting to those quiet but oh-so-informative midweek jumping fixtures at Huntingdon or Wincanton.

From the punter's point of view, a knowledge of the characteristics of individual courses can be a very important element in your armoury for the battle against the bookies. Some horses simply act better on a particular track, or a particular sort of track, than another, and identifying course specialists can be a very profitable pastime. Certain courses – Cheltenham and Sandown Park spring to mind – make demands on a horse which other, easier tracks do not, and at such places it pays to follow horses which have done well there, or at similar courses, before. When considering backing a horse in a race, never ignore what the form book tells you about which sort of course suits it.

But racing is about much more than betting, and nothing epitomises the appeal of the sport in Great Britain more than the range and variety of our racecourses. Whether your interest is mainly as a television viewer or as a racegoer – or, ideally, both! – we hope this *Channel Four Racing Guide* will prove an informative, useful and even profitable companion.

As my Channel Four mate Big Mac never tires of saying . . . Come racing!

Matters of course

From Perth in the north to Newton Abbot in the south, Yarmouth in the east to Bangor-on-Dee in the west, there are fifty-nine racecourses in Great Britain (sixty if you count separately the two courses – Rowley Mile and July Course – at Newmarket). Some stage Flat racing only, some jump racing only, and some offer both; three have all-weather tracks. There are five courses in Scotland – Ayr, Hamilton Park, Kelso, Musselburgh and Perth – and two in Wales – Bangor-on-Dee and Chepstow. The remaining fifty-two are in England.

The variety which characterises Britain's racecourses is reflected in their history. Many developed from festivals and fairs held in towns around the country – at Chester, for example, there has been racing on the Roodeye continuously since the early sixteenth century, when the race for the Silver Bell formed part of the city's Shrove Tuesday celebrations. Newmarket's position as a centre for racing and training grew out of its popularity with sporting monarchs from the early seventeenth century. Ascot took the eye of Queen Anne as a likely spot for an afternoon's sport and the first royal meeting was held in 1711. Later in the eighteenth century regular racing became established at such familiar venues as York, Doncaster and Epsom.

Originally racecourses were sited on common land. You had to pay for admission to the stands and enclosures, but outside these anyone could turn up and witness the action without charge – much as you can today at such courses as Newmarket or York. Then, late in the nineteenth century, came the notion of the 'park' course, where the whole racecourse area was enclosed within a fence and everyone paid to get in – the idea being that such a restriction would stabilise course finances (thereby improving the general level of prize money) and rid the racecourse of unruly elements. In the wake of the successful innovation at Sandown Park (see page 141) came other park courses in the London suburbs: Kempton Park at Sunbury-on-Thames opened in 1878 and Hurst Park, near Hampton Court Palace, in 1890.

Although there has been no completely new racecourse – that is, at a fresh location – since the opening of Taunton in 1927, the establishment of the all-weather courses at Southwell (opened 1989) and Wolverhampton (1993) produced what are in effect new courses: new siting, new stands and facilities, new track.

Conversely, at other courses activities are contracting. In July 1998 the British Horseracing Board announced that two courses were to give up staging National Hunt racing – Windsor from the end of 1998 and Lingfield from March 1999 – following on the heels of Nottingham, which became a Flat-only course in 1996.

Closed courses

Fifteen racecourses have closed down since the end of the Second World War:

Newport 1948	Birmingham 1965
Beaufort Hunt 1956	Rothbury 1965
Buckfastleigh 1960	Bogside 1965
Hurst Park 1962	Alexandra Park 1970
Woore 1963	Wye 1974
Manchester 1963	Lanark 1977
Lincoln 1964	Teesside Park 1981
Lewes 1964	

The course which staged the largest number of days' racing in the 1997 Flat season was Lingfield Park, with fifty-three days. The Flat courses which staged the fewest were Carlisle, Chepstow and Kempton Park, each with nine days.

In the 1997–8 National Hunt season the courses which staged the most racing were Market Rasen and Uttoxeter, each with nineteen days. Wolverhampton staged just one.

Owners and users

Racecourses are owned in a variety of ways. Ascot belongs to the Crown. Sandown Park, Kempton Park and Epsom Downs form United Racecourses, itself part of Racecourse Holdings Trust, which is owned by the Jockey Club and includes twelve courses under its banner: Aintree, Cheltenham, Haydock Park, Huntingdon, Market Rasen, Newmarket, Nottingham, Warwick and Wincanton in addition to the United Racecourses tracks. Some – such as Doncaster, Worcester and Yarmouth – are owned by the local councils. Some are owned by private companies.

Whatever their ownership, most racecourses have been undertaking major rebuilding and refurbishment in recent years, and today an essential consideration when planning new course facilities is their potential for use on non-racing days. For most racecourses, it is no longer enough to rely on horse racing alone for financial support; the optimum use of facilities – not only the stands, but the inside of the track and the surrounding land – at other times is vital. Many tracks have golf courses or caravan parks on the infield, and most use grandstand facilities for exhibitions, conferences and dinners: glass-fronted panoramic restaurants, a regular feature of greyhound tracks for many years, have recently found favour at racecourses, with the lead of the new-look Wolverhampton being followed by Cheltenham and Kempton Park. Sandown Park even has a ski-slope, discreetly concealed behind the Rhododendron Walk along which the runners walk to and from the parade ring. At the humbler end of affairs, many rural tracks regularly host car boot sales on non-racing weekends.

Horses for courses: a few examples

- Tempering won twenty-two times at Southwell
- Rapporteur won nineteen times at Lingfield Park
- Suluk won eighteen times at Southwell
- Certain Justice won fourteen times at Fontwell Park
- Manhattan Boy won fourteen times at Plumpton
- Lochranza won twelve times at Ayr
- Rapid Lad won twelve times at Beverley
- Kilbrittain Castle won eleven times at Sandown Park
- Peaty Sandy won ten times at Newcastle
- Prince Carlton won ten times at Fakenham

Horses for courses

Racecourses come in all different shapes and sizes. So do racehorses. The theory of 'horses for courses' aims to match an individual horse to its ideal racing arena.

All horses gallop, but some are known as 'galloping types' – horses whose main strength is a long, ground-devouring stride, ideally suited to a course where there are not too many undulations (as going uphill or downhill can disrupt the rhythm of the gallop) or sharp bends. The 'nippy' type, on the other hand, is likely to be physically smaller and more compact than the galloping sort, better suited to courses where balance is at a premium. In addition, some horses show a marked preference for going left-handed or right-handed.

While it is possible to glean some indication of the nature of the horse's running style simply from its physical appearance – galloping types tend to be tall, for example, and a gangly looking horse is unlikely to show exceptional balance – the notion of 'horses for courses' is best tested against the racing record, especially on the more quirky tracks.

The relentless galloper will come into his own at a course like the Rowley Mile at Newmarket, where only races over distances above one and a quarter miles involve any bend at all. The horse with the giant stride will be in his element here – and for an example think no further than that imposing chestnut Nashwan, who ate up the Rowley Mile with his raking stride when winning the 1989 Two Thousand Guineas. Imagine how he would have got on over the tight, up-and-down circuit at Folkestone . . .

One notoriously eccentric course is Epsom Downs, where the key characteristic needed is balance to come down that helter-skelter hill. Study the running of Silver Patriarch in the 1997 Derby (in which he was short-headed by Benny The Dip) and 1998 Coronation Cup (in which he beat Swain): in both cases this fine grey, essentially a galloping type, was seriously uncomfortable on the undulating part of the course, and all at sea on the descent to Tattenham Corner. But once in the straight he came into his own, and his giant stride started to eat up the ground – with varying outcomes on those two occasions.

No wonder the question 'Will he act on the course?' is asked with monotonous regularity of every decent candidate during the run-up to the Derby, and no wonder some owners – notably, in recent years, Peter Savill with Celtic Swing in 1995 – decline to aim their horse at the Blue Riband once convinced that, however prestigious the race, the horse will not act on the track. You can never be entirely sure of this until the individual has tried it, of course, but as well as the general style of running there are clues to be had in a horse's conformation: for example, an animal with an over-straight knee, or one in which the pasterns, the shock absorbers between the foot and the leg, do not have much of a slope, is thought to be unlikely to keep his balance when going steeply downhill, and may be best avoided at a course like Epsom.

'Horses for courses' applies just as much over jumps. Red Rum was in his element over the Grand National course, and was three times winner and twice runner-up in five outings there. At the other end of the prestige scale, following course specialists at awkward tracks like Plumpton or Fontwell Park can prove highly profitable.

Indeed, from the punter's point of view, the most obvious application of the 'horses for courses' notion is to back a horse that has won on the course before, on the simple basis that if he's done it once he must have what it takes to act on that track, and so might

Racecourse statues

Many of the true greats among racehorses have been
acknowledged by statues gracing the sites of their exploits.
A few examples are:

- Red Rum at Aintree and at Ayr
- Arkle, Dawn Run and Golden Miller at Cheltenham
- Desert Orchid at Kempton Park
- Brigadier Gerard and Eclipse at Newmarket
- Generous at Epsom Downs

A small bronze of Brown Jack is displayed at Ascot each year on
the day of the Brown Jack Stakes . . . Goodwood has an Elizabeth
Frink bronze of an unnamed horse . . . Hyperion, by John Skeaping,
stands outside the Jockey Club Rooms at Newmarket.

Overseas statues include those of:

- Gladiateur at Longchamp
- Vintage Crop at The Curragh
- Secretariat at Belmont Park

well oblige again. A previous course win is indicated on racecards
and race programmes in the newspapers by the letter 'C' against
the horse's name. 'C,D' means that the horse has won not only on
that course, but over the distance of that race – somewhere else;
'CD' – has won over that distance at that course – is even more
persuasive, and one of the more logical betting systems (one that
even Big Mac favours) is to back a horse that has won the same race
in the past.

Always take into account evidence of whether a horse prefers a
left-handed or right-handed track. It's usually simply that it feels
more comfortable turning in one direction or the other, but there's
an additional factor with jumpers, as a horse who tends to jump to
the left would be better off on a left-handed track. A famous

example of a horse with a preference for one direction is Desert Orchid, who was significantly better right-handed than left-handed. He may have had his finest hour in the 1989 Cheltenham Gold Cup on a left-handed track, but only two of his thirty-four career victories were gained going anti-clockwise. (Turf trivia time: where was the other one? . . . The answer is on page 32.)

Going

Most major punters – Channel Four Racing's Jim McGrath among them – will tell you that one of the essential considerations when picking a winner is the state of the ground: in racing parlance, the 'going'. If a horse does not act on the ground prevailing on the day, forget it – but be careful to satisfy yourself about the evidence: it is one thing to know that the horse has never won on the going, but has he actually run poorly on it?

For racing on turf, there are seven official states of the going:

- hard
- firm
- good to firm
- good
- good to soft
- soft
- heavy

For all-weather racing (see page 22) there are just three categories:

- fast
- standard
- slow

The clerk of the course will give advance assessments of the state of the ground (published in the racing press) in the few days leading up to each meeting to alert trainers to likely conditions, and will declare the official going on the day – though this can alter during the programme, for example in the case of a torrential downpour.

The top Flat races by course

Twenty-five Group One races on the Flat were scheduled to be run in Britain in 1998:

Seven at Newmarket
  Two Thousand Guineas
  One Thousand Guineas
  July Cup
  Middle Park Stakes
  Cheveley Park Stakes
  Champion Stakes
  Dewhurst Stakes

Six at Ascot
  St James's Palace Stakes
  Coronation Stakes
  Gold Cup
  King George VI and Queen
    Elizabeth Diamond Stakes
  Queen Elizabeth II Stakes
  Fillies' Mile

Three at Epsom Downs
  Oaks
  Derby
  Coronation Cup

Three at York
  International Stakes
  Yorkshire Oaks
  Nunthorpe Stakes

Two at Doncaster
  St Leger
  Racing Post Trophy

One at Goodwood
  Sussex Stakes

One at Haydock Park
  Sprint Cup

One at Newbury
  Lockinge Stakes

One at Sandown Park
  Eclipse Stakes

Normally one category will cover the course, though sometimes the official statement will allow for variations on different parts of the track: for example, 'Good, good to soft in the back straight'.

The going is usually measured by the traditional method of the clerk of the course shoving a stick into the ground, though some courses supplement gut feeling with a numerical reading obtained by using the Penetrometer, a device developed in France whereby a weight is dropped down a metal rod at various parts of the course. Some trainers complain that some clerks of the course give misleading information on going in order to encourage connections to run their horses (for example, a trainer of the average chaser is

---

The top National Hunt races by course

Over jumps, there were twenty-five Grade One races in the 1997–8 programme:

Eleven at Cheltenham
    Cleeve Hurdle
    Supreme Novices' Hurdle
    Arkle Chase
    Champion Hurdle
    Royal & SunAlliance Novices'
      Hurdle
    Queen Mother Champion
      Chase
    Royal & SunAlliance Novices'
      Chase
    Champion Bumper
    Triumph Hurdle
    Stayers' Hurdle
    Cheltenham Gold Cup

Four at Aintree
    Maghull Novices' Chase
    Melling Chase
    Sefton Novices' Hurdle
    Aintree Hurdle

Three at Sandown Park
    Tingle Creek Chase
    Tolworth Novices' Hurdle
    Scilly Isles Novices' Chase

Three at Kempton Park
    Feltham Novices' Chase
    King George VI Chase
    Christmas Hurdle

Two at Ascot
    Long Walk Hurdle
    Comet Chase

One at Chepstow
    Finale Junior Hurdle

One at Newbury
    Challow Hurdle

---

more likely to run his horse if the going is good to soft than if it is good to firm); the Jockey Club's instruction to courses is that they should aim – though naturally, given the climate, they can do no more than aim – to produce good ground for jump racing and good to firm for Flat racing.

Most courses now use some artificial means of watering to help produce the desired ground – either portable sprays or an in-built system whereby jets of water are played on to different parts of the course. The trouble with watering, of course, is that just as you switch off the system, it starts to rain . . .

All-weather racing

All-weather racing – horse racing on artificial surfaces as opposed to grass – crept up on a mostly indifferent racing public when Niklas Angel won the William Hill Claiming Stakes at Lingfield Park on 30 October 1989. The following day saw the first all-weather fixture at Southwell, and four years later the two pioneer courses were joined by Wolverhampton: the first fixture there on 27 December 1993 included two races under floodlights, the first illuminated horse races in Britain.

While racing on artificial surfaces has long been a feature of the sport overseas (in North America, for example, races on turf are comparatively unusual), there had been resistance to the notion in Britain. But in the early 1980s there was increasing concern – especially in the betting industry – about the number of fixtures being lost to adverse weather in the depths of winter: no racing meant significantly less business in betting shops, and turnover took a dive. January and February 1985 saw no fewer than seventy-two days' scheduled racing lost to the climate, and the Jockey Club launched an investigation into the feasibility of a limited amount of all-weather sport. In November 1985 the go-ahead was given, the carefully laid plans coming to fruition at Lingfield Park at eleven o'clock on a Monday morning nearly four years later.

Sheikh Mohammed had his first British winner on the all-weather on 3 March 1995 when Warluskee won the Skegby Maiden Stakes at Southwell.

It was not all plain sailing. Ironically, some early fixtures were lost to the weather – fog was a hazard whatever the surface, and one Lingfield fixture was abandoned after the approach roads to the course were snow-bound – but gradually all-weather racing on the Flat became an accepted (if not especially glamorous) version of the sport.

Attempts at all-weather jump racing were short-lived. Jockeys disliked the lack of 'give' in the surface, which could make falls – for horses and riders alike – more painful and more serious than the same accidents would have been on turf. Adverse publicity was attracted by a spate of equine deaths on all-weather tracks, and all-weather jumping was suspended in February 1994. It never came back.

All-weather racing has had a significant effect on the shape of the racing year, since the official Flat season now begins on 1 January and ends on 31 December; in the old days, there would have been no Flat racing before Doncaster in March or after the middle of November. This transformation has exercised statisticians and caused controversy about such matters as the period over which the jockeys' championship runs, but much more significant is the way in which racing on artificial surfaces is now woven into the whole of the year, rather than taking place only when the weather is at its most inclement in the bleak midwinter. In 1997, for example, there were 126 all-weather fixtures, nearly one-fifth of the total Flat days that year.

Racing surfaces on the three all-weather tracks are made from compounds of specially graded sand stabilized with synthetic fibres: Lingfield Park uses a substance called Equitrack, while Southwell's and Wolverhampton's are Fibresand.

Technicalities

Technology – a crucially important facet of every racecourse in the interests of fairness – is handled in Britain by RaceTech, a subsidiary of the Racecourse Association which is responsible for the key areas of technical support.

Starting stalls

Starting stalls – used only on the Flat – ensure that all runners get an equal break at the start of a race. Long in use in other major racing countries, they were first employed in Britain on 8 July 1965 on the July Course at Newmarket: Track Spare became the first winner of a race started from stalls when landing the Chesterfield Stakes under Lester Piggott. The first English Classic started by stalls was the 1967 Derby, won by Royal Palace.

Stalls come in ten-bay units which are manoeuvred around the racecourse and transported from course to course by a fleet of modified Land Rovers (though in the spring of 1998 Wolverhampton became the first course to have its own, specially designed stalls; see page 171). At each meeting the stalls are supported by a team of nine professional horse handlers whose role is to load the horses as efficiently as possible. The bays are designed so that the handler can lead the horse in and then duck out under the front gates. Within each stall are narrow shelves to the side on which the jockey may stand to take the weight off the horse's back while other runners are being loaded.

Before runners enter the stalls, the front gates are locked in a closed position; at the moment of starting they are all opened simultaneously by an electrical release mechanism operated by the starter.

Photo finish

The photo finish was first used in Great Britain to decide second and third places in the Great Metropolitan Handicap at Epsom in April 1947, and first used in a Classic to unravel the 1949 Two Thousand Guineas: Nimbus by a short head from Abernant. Later in 1949 Nimbus was again judged the winner in the first photo-finish Derby – by a head from Amour Drake with Swallow Tail another head away third.

Photo-finish technology is based on the idea of photographing the finishers on to moving film through a very narrow aperture as they cross the line, so that the image is essentially one of time (the time taken for each horse to cross the line), not an orthodox photograph.

Two cameras are usually used – one to cover the whole width of the track and the other concentrating on the far side, where horses may be obscured by other runners nearer the first camera. The camera has a vertical adjustable slit (minimum aperture fourthousandths of an inch), and the film speed is adjusted depending on the expected speed of the finishers (which is why a horse crossing the line very slowly will appear elongated on the photograph). Film and prints were originally monochrome, but colour (which makes for more accurate decisions) is now in regular use.

As soon as the last runner in a race has passed the post, the film is quickly developed and the image transmitted on to a monitor in the judge's box, where it can be enlarged up to six times if necessary. An additional aid, first used at Goodwood in May 1995, is Hawkeye, the computerised system which allows the judge instantaneous access to the image.

The judge names the official distances from measuring the photo-finish strip.

Timing

When the starter presses the button which releases the front gates of the starting stalls, he or she automatically activates the electronic timing system, and the time at which each horse crosses the line at the winning post is plotted on the photo-finish strip.

Electronic sectional timing – timing the runners in a race over each segment of the distance – has been experimented with in Britain over the last few years and is now in operation on the Rowley Mile at Newmarket: hence the timings which appear on the television screen during Channel Four races on that track.

Camera patrol

Cameras situated around the course, directed from RaceTech's mobile on-course control unit, record every race from all sorts of different angles to provide video coverage for post-race scrutiny by the stewards (and for television viewers). Camera patrols were first used in Britain in 1960.

Obstacles

Steeplechase fences (other than water jumps) must not be lower than four feet six inches high. They are usually constructed of birch packed into a wooden frame, with a sloped apron of gorse on the take-off side, and a horizontal board along the ground painted to give a 'groundline' by which the horse will judge when to take off. An open ditch incorporates a ditch protected by a low rail on the take-off side. (The fences on the Grand National course at Aintree are built from thorn dressed with spruce.)

Hurdles are on most courses like sheep hurdles, with gorse and birch woven into a wooden frame driven into the ground. The distance from the top bar to the ground must be not less than three feet six inches. At Southwell and Wolverhampton hurdle races take place over obstacles quite different from the traditional type and much like little chase fences, with plastic birch packed into a frame, sloped on the take-off side. The theory is that such obstacles encourage better jumping than the usual form of hurdle, which can be knocked out of the ground.

People

It takes a large number of people to stage a race meeting.
Permanent racecourse staff include:

- *the clerk of the course*, who bears sole responsibility to the stewards for the general arrangement of the meeting, and whose duties broadly cover the conduct of the fixture, including the condition of the course, the framing of the racing programme, going reports (often a contentious area with trainers) and other matters relating directly to the racing itself;
- *the racecourse manager*, who administers the use of the course both for racing and for other purposes but has no formal responsibility to the stewards;
- *ground staff* who look after the racing surface (a highly skilled and important job) as well as the fences, rails, etc.

Jockey Club officials include:

- the stewards, whose basic role is to apply the Rules of Racing;
- the starter;
- the judge;
- the clerk of the scales, who oversees the weighing-in and weighing-out of jockeys;
- flagmen, veterinary officers, Jockey Club security officers, etc.

Casual workers drafted in for the day include catering staff, car park attendants, gate stewards and security personnel.

Police oversee traffic, crowd behaviour, and so on.

And then there are the racegoers . . .

Attendances

Total attendance at the 1,118 days at the races in 1997 was just over five million, at an average of about 4,500 per day.

The race watched in the flesh by the greatest number of spectators is still the Derby at Epsom Downs, but as thousands of Derby Day revellers watch the race from the Downs rather than pay to go in the enclosures, the exact figure cannot be known. Estimated attendance at the 1998 Derby won by High-Rise was 100,000.

Derby Day apart, 1998 also saw especially large numbers of paying spectators at:

- Ascot on Gold Cup day, with 67,272;
- Cheltenham on Tote Gold Cup day, with 50,300 (total attendance at the three days of the National Hunt Festival in 1998 was 140,123);
- Aintree on Martell Grand National day, with 46,182.
- Ascot on King George VI and Queen Elizabeth Diamond Stakes day, with 32,611.

All big occasions, but consider this. On Spring Bank Holiday Monday 1997, no fewer than 21,000 racegoers cheerfully squeezed themselves into the tiny Lake District course of Cartmel – which just goes to show that not everyone visits a racecourse with the intention of watching horses race.

Flat

National Hunt

Flat and National Hunt

A/W: all-weather track

Perth ●

● **Musselburgh**

Hamilton Park ●

Kelso ●

Ayr

Newcastle ●

Carlisle ● *Hexham* ●

Sedgefield ● Redcar ●

Catterick ●

Cartmel ● Thirsk ●

Ripon ● York ●

Wetherby ●

Pontefract ● Beverley ●

Aintree ● **Doncaster** ● *Market Rasen* ●

Haydock Park ●

Chester ● ● **Southwell** A/W

Bangor-on-Dee ● Nottingham ● *Fakenham* ●

Uttoxeter ● Yarmouth

Wolverhampton A/W ● ● **Leicester** *Huntingdon* ●

Ludlow ● **Warwick** ●

Worcester ● *Stratford* ● Newmarket ●

Hereford ● *Towcester* ●

Cheltenham ●

Chepstow ● **Windsor** **Kempton Park**

Newbury **Ascot** ● ● **Sandown Park**

Bath ● ● **Lingfield Park** A/W

Salisbury ● Epsom Downs ●

Taunton ● Goodwood ● *Plumpton* ● ● **Folkestone**

Wincanton ● *Fontwell Park* ●

Exeter ●

Brighton

Newton Abbot ●

The racecourses of Great Britain

The following pages provide an account of the nature of each of Britain's fifty-nine racecourses, along with a small amount of very basic information designed to help you plan your day at the races. If you need to know further details – for example, regarding crèches or other family facilities, special arrangements for the disabled, admission prices for a particular day, group bookings or whatever – do not hesitate to contact the course directly and enquire. Telephone and, where available, fax numbers and e-mail addresses are given for each course; the racing world is quickly embracing the new technology, and many now have Internet websites, which contain all sorts of information about fixtures, booking arrangements, hospitality, non-racing activities and so on; with some you can actually book through the Internet.

For each of the Flat tracks we have provided a simple expression of the perceived effect of the draw (the position in the starting stalls allotted to each horse) on that course. This can be an important factor when assessing races – especially over short distances – but it should be remembered that the effect of the draw is not written in stone: on some courses the influence of a particular draw depends on factors such as the state of the going or the position of the stalls, and on others the effect of the draw remains a matter of opinion. Study the racing press – or better still listen to Channel Four Racing's resident experts – for the latest up-to-date information.

In the course plans of steeplechase tracks, 'OD' signifies an open ditch, 'W' the water jump; fences without any such abbreviation are plain fences.

Aintree

National Hunt only, left-handed

Address Aintree Racecourse, Ormskirk Road, Aintree, Liverpool L9 5AS
Telephone 0151 523 2600
Fax 0151 522 2920
E-mail aintree@races.u-net.com
Web www.demon.co.uk/racenews/aintree

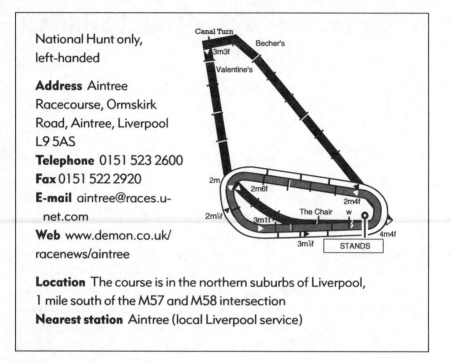

Location The course is in the northern suburbs of Liverpool, 1 mile south of the M57 and M58 intersection
Nearest station Aintree (local Liverpool service)

Becher's Brook, the Chair, Valentine's Brook, the Melling Road, the Elbow – Aintree is the most familiar of all racecourses, its landmarks known to millions outside racing whose experience of the sport extends no further than one race: the Grand National.

There are two distinct circuits.

The Grand National course is two and a quarter miles round, the longest circuit of any British racecourse, and completely flat. In the National – the longest race in the calendar, run over four and a half miles and thirty fences – the runners start at the beginning of the long, wide straight leading away from the stands. On the two-furlong run to the first fence they cross the Melling Road (Melling was a village next to Aintree), then negotiate five obstacles – the third of which is a gigantic open ditch – before coming to Becher's Brook, the sixth on the first circuit. The problem with Becher's is not so much its height as the very marked drop on the landing side. Immediately on landing over Becher's the runners turn left towards the seventh, the apparently innocuous plain fence which becomes the twenty-third on the second circuit – and which in 1967 was the site of the infamous pile-up which let Foinavon through to Grand National immortality at 100–1. The eighth on the first circuit is the Canal Turn, which immediately precedes a ninety-degree left-handed turn. Then comes a sequence of four fences in quick succession – Valentine's Brook, plain fence, open ditch, plain fence – before the field crosses the Melling Road again and swings left-handed to face the thirteenth and fourteenth, both plain fences.

In front of the stands the course narrows on the approach to the fifteenth: the Chair, five feet two inches high and preceded by a yawning six-foot ditch. (The name derives from the distance judge's chair, which in ages past was situated 240 yards from the winning post: the black iron pedestal which supported it is still there.) The Chair is the moment of truth in any Grand National: get that far and clear that daunting obstacle, and you're in with a real chance.

Next comes the water jump, then the sweeping left-handed turn past the starting point and out again on that run to Becher's (which second time round is the twenty-second fence); on to the Canal Turn (twenty-fourth), left to Valentine's (twenty-fifth), then those three fences before crossing the Melling Road for the last time and facing up to the last two – and then the seemingly endless run-in of 494 yards, halfway along which the horses tack to the right at the Elbow to bypass the Chair and water jump. No winning post is ever more welcome than this one.

Injuries to riders at Aintree – Tim Brookshaw in a hurdle race and Paddy Farrell at the Chair in the Grand National – led to the establishment in 1964 of a charity which grew into the Injured Jockeys' Fund.

The Grand National is the highlight of the three-day Aintree festival meeting in early April, and the National course is used for big races on each of the other days: the John Hughes Trophy (commemorating one of the great clerks of the course) over two and three-quarter miles on the Thursday, and the Fox Hunters' Chase (two and three-quarter miles) for hunter-chasers on the Friday.

Several other important races are run at this very high-quality meeting. They include the Martell Cup (three miles one furlong) – Desert Orchid's victory in the 1988 running, the twentieth of his career, was his first on a left-handed track; the Melling Chase (two and a half miles), which in 1998 saw the tragic end of One Man just sixteen days after his moment of Cheltenham glory in the Queen Mother Champion Chase; and the Aintree Hurdle (two and a half miles), a natural follow-up for Champion Hurdle horses: 1998 Champion Hurdler Istabraq was just touched off by Pridwell in 1998, and previous winners of the race have included the likes of Comedy Of Errors, Monksfield (three times, including a famous dead heat with Night Nurse in 1977), Gaye Brief, Dawn Run, Beech Road, Morley Street (three times) and Danoli (twice).

Red Rum ran his first race at Liverpool, dead-heating in the Thursby Selling Plate over five furlongs for two-year-olds on 7 April 1967. The only horse ever to have won three Grand Nationals, he died at the age of thirty in 1995 and is now buried by the winning post at the course.

These three races are all run on the Mildmay Course, at one and a half miles round a much sharper proposition than the National circuit. The final two bends are tight, and horses tend to go very fast round here, making it a course for the fast, nippy type, whereas the National course very much favours the galloper – and the Grand National itself demands bold, accurate jumping and buckets of stamina besides.

On the Mildmay Course the steeplechase fences are constructed in the orthodox way from birch, while on the Grand National course they are built from thorn dressed with spruce.

In 1992 the November meeting, which had been abandoned some years previously, was revived: the major race at that meeting is the

Becher Handicap Chase, run over three miles three furlongs of the National course.

There was racing in the Liverpool area in the sixteenth century, though the contest which became the Grand National did not begin life until the 1830s. The earliest years of the great race remain the subject of debate among racing anoraks, but there is no disputing that 'The Grand Liverpool Steeplechase' was run at Aintree in 1839, 'four miles across country', the conditions including the stipulation: 'no rider to open a gate or ride through a gateway, or more than 100 yards along any road, footpath or driftway'. The race was won by Lottery, and by the time he had crossed the winning line one of the obstacles, described as 'a strong paling, next a rough, high jagged hedge, and lastly a brook about six feet wide', had entered racing lore. On the first circuit a horse named Conrad had hit the 'paling' very hard and dumped his jockey in the brook. Pausing to observe that 'water is no damned use without brandy', the jockey remounted, only to get dunked again at the next brook (now Valentine's). Conrad's rider was one Captain Martin Becher, and thus Becher's Brook – a phrase which has entered the language to mean a particularly difficult obstacle – was christened.

The last Flat race meeting at Liverpool was held on 1 April 1976.

Aintree has had its ups and downs since the Second World War, and great uncertainty over the course's future during changes of ownership in the 1960s and 1970s led to the gradual dilapidation of facilities: it was ironic that the greatest National performance of modern times, that of Crisp in 1973, came in a running of the race which many expected to be the last. But in 1975 Ladbrokes came to the rescue, running the course on a seven-year lease until 1982, when a public appeal was launched; eventually – not least through the good offices of one John McCririck as honest broker when negotiations had stalled – the course reached the safe haven of ownership by the Jockey Club, and is now under the umbrella of Racecourse Holdings Trust.

From those dark days when it seemed odds-on that the historic Grand National course would disappear into the hands of property developers, Aintree has staged a remarkable recovery, and the Grand National Festival is the biggest fixture of the jumping year after Cheltenham. The Queen Mother Stand was opened in 1991 alongside the old and elegant County Stand, and the Princess Royal Stand, replacing the old grandstand, in 1998.

Tommo's tip . . .
'Don't stay in the grandstand to watch the Grand National. Go in the middle of the course and wander around to see the excitement of the world's greatest steeplechase in front of your very eyes.'

Ascot

Flat and National Hunt, right-handed

Address Ascot Racecourse, Ascot, Berkshire SL5 7JN
Telephone 01344 622211
Fax 01344 628299
E-mail ascot@itl.net
Web www.sportinglife.co.uk/ascot/

Location Ascot is 6 miles south-west of Windsor, 3 miles east
of Bracknell, with easy access from both the M3 (junction 3) and
M4 (junctions 6 or 7)
Nearest station Ascot (on the London Waterloo–Reading line),
10 minutes' walk from course

Effect of the draw Low numbers favoured on the straight course
in soft going

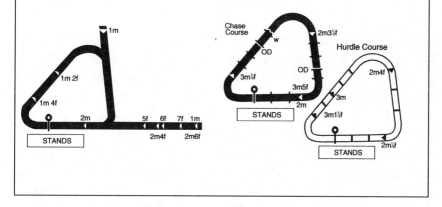

'Ascot': the very word sums up images of toppers and morning dress,
high fashion and silly hats, the Royal Family in their carriage procession up the royal course – and, for true racing aficionados, the best
four days of Flat racing anywhere in the world.

But Ascot racecourse has much more to offer than just the Royal
Meeting in mid-June. Throughout the year, under both Flat and
National Hunt codes, Ascot provides sport of a consistently high
quality in surroundings which reflect its royal connections.

That connection goes back to 1711, when Queen Anne, the ample-girthed forty-six-year-old monarch, was taking a carriage ride through the forest near Windsor Castle and came upon a large clearing. Immediately registering that this was the ideal place to indulge her love of equestrian sport (though she was by then too stout to follow the family tradition and ride in races herself), she ordered the clearing to be prepared for horse racing, and the next time the court was in Windsor that summer, racing at Ascot was under way – with 'Her Majesty's Plate of 100 guineas' on 11 August 1711. Today the founder of the course is commemorated in the opening race of the Royal Meeting: the Queen Anne Stakes.

The Queen Alexandra Stakes, final race of the Royal Meeting, is the longest Flat race in the calendar: two miles six furlongs thirty-four yards.

From that beginning, Ascot developed through the eighteenth century into one of the major racing venues in the land, and the Royal Meeting into one of the great social occasions of the year. George IV instituted the tradition of the carriage procession up the course in 1825, by which time the Gold Cup was firmly established as the principal race at Ascot, having been first run in 1807.

The Gold Cup is run over two and a half miles (the longest Group One race of the season in Britain) on the third afternoon of the four-day Royal Meeting. Gold Cup day – 'Ladies' Day' – remains the social pinnacle of the week, but for racing purists the key events of Royal Ascot are the earlier Group One races: the St James's Palace Stakes for three-year-old colts over the round mile (known at Ascot as the 'Old Mile') on the Tuesday, and the Coronation Stakes, the equivalent race for three-year-old fillies, on the Wednesday.

Although elevated to Group One status only as recently as 1988, the St James's Palace Stakes is now the most valuable race of the Royal Meeting; in 1998 the victorious Dr Fong netted £138,900 for his owners, the Thoroughbred Corporation. The prospect of rich pickings on this scale makes the race a regular port of call for horses who have figured prominently in the Two Thousand Guineas

(English, Irish or French variety) earlier in the season – though the last winner of the Two Thousand Guineas at Newmarket to win the race was To-Agori-Mou in 1981, following in the hoofsteps of such greats as Tudor Minstrel and Brigadier Gerard.

Similarly, the Coronation Stakes has close connections with the One Thousand Guineas: since the war, eight winners of the fillies' Classic at Newmarket have won the Royal Ascot race.

It was at Ascot on 28 September 1996 that Frankie Dettori became the first jockey in racing history to go through a seven-race card. His winners were Wall Street, Diffident, Mark Of Esteem, Decorated Hero, Fatefully, Lochangel and Fujiyama Crest.

But the great appeal of Royal Ascot as a race meeting is the overall quality of the fare, with those three Group One events taking their place alongside many other major races:

- the Royal Hunt Cup (straight mile) and Wokingham Stakes (six furlongs), highly competitive handicaps which form the major betting mediums of the week;
- high-class sprint races in the King's Stand Stakes (five furlongs) and Cork and Orrery Stakes (six furlongs);
- major two-year-old races such as the Coventry Stakes (six furlongs) and, for fillies, the Queen Mary Stakes (five furlongs);
- major middle-distance races for three-year-olds over a mile and a half: the King Edward VII Stakes (colts and geldings) and Ribblesdale Stakes (fillies);
- high-class Group Two events for three-year-olds and older in the Queen Anne Stakes (straight mile) and Prince of Wales's Stakes (one and a quarter miles);
- the Hardwicke Stakes (one and a half miles) for four-year-olds and upwards aspiring to the top rank of middle-distance horses.

Quality is the watchword for the rest of the Ascot year too.

The King George VI and Queen Elizabeth Diamond Stakes, run over one and a half miles in late July, is arguably – whatever may be claimed of the Derby – the single most important Flat race of the year in this country, attracting the top horses from different generations and invariably an event of the highest class. For example, between the inaugural race in 1951 and the forty-eighth running in 1998, the King George has been won twelve times by the winner of the same year's Derby (Tulyar, Pinza, Nijinsky, Mill Reef, Grundy, The Minstrel, Troy, Shergar, Reference Point, Nashwan, Generous and Lammtarra), twice by Derby winners later in their careers (Royal Palace and Teenoso) and by many other greats such as Dahlia and Swain (the only two horses to have won the race twice), Ribot, Ballymoss, Ragusa, Park Top, Brigadier Gerard, Time Charter, Dancing Brave and Mtoto.

Racegoers at Royal Ascot in 1998 consumed:

- 196,000 bottles of champagne
- 2.5 tonnes of beef
- 2.2 tonnes of smoked salmon
- 6,000 lobsters
- 4 tonnes of strawberries
- 520 gallons of cream
- 70,000 bottles of wine
- 11,000 bottles of Pimms

The other two Group One races at Ascot are both run over the Old Mile at the Ascot Festival in late September: the Queen Elizabeth II Stakes for three-year-olds and upwards, and the Fillies' Mile for two-year-old fillies, a race which since its founding in 1973 has indicated the Classic potential of such winners as Quick As Lightning, Oh So Sharp, Diminuendo, Bosra Sham and Reams Of Verse. The September meeting also has the Royal Lodge Stakes (Group Two) over the round mile for staying two-year-olds.

National Hunt racing at Ascot began in April 1965, the new track having received a turf transplant from Hurst Park, which had closed down in 1962. For some racegoers jump racing here lacks immediacy and the true excitement of the winter game at its best, as the chase and hurdles courses are inside the Flat track, and thus somewhat remote from the stands: jumping at Ascot has been famously described as 'like Blackpool with the tide out'. But, as on the Flat, the standard of racing is very high. Principal events include the Victor Chandler Chase (two miles) in January; the Comet Chase (two miles three and a half furlongs) in February, won in 1998 by One Man; the First National Bank Gold Cup (two miles three and a half furlongs) in November, and the Long Walk Hurdle and Betterware Gold Cup Chase (both three miles) in December. The last-named began life in 1965 as the SGB Chase, and under that name the following year was the last race ever won by the immortal Arkle.

Brough Scott rode his last winner under Rules at Ascot: Kitaab in the Shadwell Estates Private Handicap on 25 September 1992. It was Brough's first winner for twenty-one years. John Oaksey finished fourth on Kabayil in the same race, his last ride under Rules in Britain: 'As we turned into the straight I looked up and the winning post appeared to be about four miles away. I realised then it was time to hang up my riding boots.'

The reason why Ascot attracts such quality under both codes lies in the nature of the course itself, a wide track with good sweeping bends. The circuit is in the shape of a right-handed triangle about a mile and six furlongs round, on to which runs the straight mile (on which are run all races shorter than a mile); the Old Mile starts on a spur and takes in one bend into the home straight. The run from the home turn is less than three furlongs, and Ascot is no course for a jockey to be well off the pace turning in – as plenty have found to their cost.

From the long bend beyond the winning post, the round course makes a gentle uphill rise and then sweeps downhill, which makes this a particularly telling part of the course for steeplechasers, who on that stretch have to negotiate two plain fences and a very trappy open ditch before the ground levels out approaching the water jump.

At the end of that straight the runners reach Swinley Bottom, where the course sweeps round to join the Old Mile and make a steadily uphill run. The ground levels out at the home turn, then rises towards the winning post before falling shortly before the line. The straight mile begins slightly downhill then undulates gently until joining the round course.

Despite that short home straight, Ascot is very much a course for the galloping type, for there are no sudden gradients to unbalance a horse. When the ground is heavy Ascot puts a strong emphasis on stamina, and in any conditions it is a track where the horse needs to get the trip well.

The old practice of ringing a bell as the Ascot runners approach the straight – to warn wandering racegoers to clear the course – is still followed today.

After years when racegoers of less distinguished breeding than the horses were made to feel like irritating intruders, under its recent enlightened management Ascot has been transformed into a far more user-friendly environment. Facilities are first-rate, the large stands and generous surrounding areas providing a sense of space lacking at many other courses. There is even a bandstand, location for many an informal sing-song at the end of a gruelling afternoon's sport in the summer sunshine. But the same sense of space can make Ascot feel somewhat bleak and cavernous in the late-afternoon chill of midwinter, when the last race is run in semi-darkness.

The parade ring for National Hunt meetings is in front of the grandstand; for summer fixtures the spacious and leafy paddock beyond the stands is used, and the pre-parade ring beyond that is an especially good place for having a long look at the runners. To lean on the rail there before the 1997 running of the King George and see walking quietly around before you the very cream of the world's racehorses – Pilsudski, Singspiel, Helissio and Swain – was an experience for the racing connoisseur.

And where is the racing connoisseur in more fitting surroundings than Ascot?

Ayr

Flat and National Hunt, left-handed

Address Ayr Racecourse, Whitletts Road, Ayr KA8 0JE
Telephone 01292 264179
Fax 01292 610140
E-mail info@ayr-racecourse.co.uk
Web www.ayr-racecourse.co.uk

Location Ayr is about 35 miles south-west of Glasgow; the racecourse is on the eastern side of the town, just off the A77
Nearest station Ayr, 1 mile from racecourse (bus to course)

Effect of the draw High numbers favoured in big fields on the straight course, especially when the going is soft

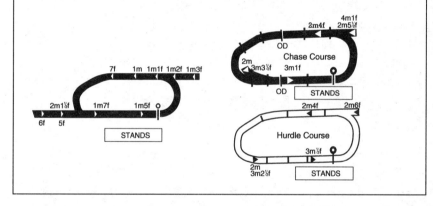

Two events dominate the racing year at Ayr, and they could hardly be more different.

The Scottish Grand National, run in April as the jumping season enters its twilight weeks, is a steeplechase over four miles one furlong – nearly three complete circuits of the course – and invariably a competitive event for top-class chasers. Red Rum won this just three weeks after beating L'Escargot to land his second triumph in the Grand National in 1974 (John Oaksey was second on Proud Tarquin). Other Grand National winners to have landed the Ayr marathon since Red Rum are Little Polveir (1987) and

Earth Summit (1994), though unlike Rummy they both won at Ayr before their moment of Liverpool glory. Merryman II, Grand National winner in 1960, won the Scottish National in 1959 at Bogside: the race moved to Ayr for the 1966 running after Bogside closed down.

Ayr's other great race is on the Flat: the Ayr Gold Cup over six furlongs, with a very large field of bullet-fast handicappers powering down the straight. That there is a Be Friendly bar at Ayr is a clue to just one of the great sprinters who have taken this race. Others include the gigantic Roman Warrior, who humped ten stone when winning by a short head from Lochnager in 1975, and the flying filly Lochsong, who started at 10–1 under Francis Arrowsmith as a four-year-old in 1992; she had already won the Stewards' Cup and the Portland Handicap that year, and the following year moved up into Group company to proclaim herself one of the finest sprinters of the modern era.

The circuit at Ayr is a left-handed oval of about a mile and a half round, with mild undulations but suitable for the long-striding, galloping sort of horse. On the Flat, five- and six-furlong races are straight and start from a spur, and the run from the home turn is half a mile. The hurdle and chase courses are inside the Flat, but similarly favour the long-striding horse.

The only time an English Classic has been run outside England was when the 1989 St Leger was transferred from Doncaster to Ayr after subsidence in the track caused the abandonment of the meeting at the Yorkshire course.

The facilities at Ayr are excellent – spacious stands, plenty of roomy bars – and the atmosphere friendly; even on the biggest days racegoers do not feel overcrowded. One particularly attractive feature for patrons of the members' enclosure nestles among the trees at the far end of the paddock – Western House, which must be just about the most civilised racecourse building in the country, housing bars and restaurants but with the feel of a large country house.

Racing on the current site dates from 1907 – the lovely old grand-stand built then remains a feature of the course – though horses were raced at Ayr as long ago as the sixteenth century.

Modern developments include a new weighing room, first used in 1995, and the Princess Royal Stand, opened the following year.

Bangor-on-Dee

National Hunt only, left-handed

Address The Racecourse, Bangor-on-Dee, near Wrexham, Clwyd
LL13 0DA
Telephone 01978 780323
Fax 01978 780985

Location Bangor-on-Dee is 22 miles north of Shrewsbury and
about 5 miles south-east of Wrexham, on the B5069
Nearest station Wrexham, 6 miles from course

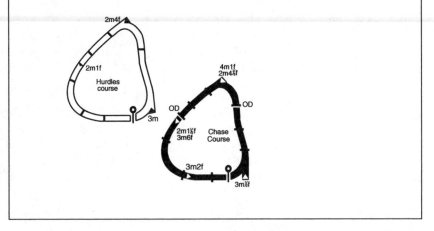

Apart from being one of the quintessential 'gaff' tracks – those small
courses which form the backbone of National Hunt racing in Britain
– Bangor-on-Dee has two perverse claims to fame: it is the only
racecourse in the country which has no building which even
purports to be a grandstand; and it is not the other Bangor in North
Wales, the university town near Anglesey. Tradition has it that many
a horsebox driver has merrily driven his charges to the latter Bangor,
only to discover his mistake too late to get to the course in time.

The lack of a grandstand does not represent a serious hardship for
Bangor-on-Dee racegoers, as they can enjoy excellent vantage points
on the hill which slopes down towards the track. None the less,
watching a race from the paddock area at Bangor can be a curious

Lesley Graham's favourite . . .

'Bangor-on-Dee was the first racecourse I ever went to – as a three-year-old – and thirty-five years on it hasn't lost its wonderfully welcoming atmosphere. When I first went racing there the course was virtually without running rails, and you had to be careful to pick your way around the cowpats! Bangor has moved with the times and is nowadays much smarter, but it's still a great place for a really relaxed, enjoyable and reasonably priced day out.'

experience as your main view of the finish is head-on. For a decent side-on view you need to take up position in the large picnic area beyond the course buildings.

The circuit is about one and a half miles round. Its sharp bends and mostly level terrain favour the nippy sort of horse rather than the relentless galloper, and it can pay to follow previous course winners here.

Fred Archer, one of the greatest jockeys of all time, rode the first winner of his career in a steeplechase at Bangor in 1869. Aged twelve (the same age as Lester Piggott was when he rode his first winner), Archer weighed out at four stone eleven pounds before winning on Maid Of Trent.

While it would be stretching a point to claim that the course stages any major races, quality of sport is not everything, and Bangor-on-Dee is a highly enjoyable place to experience the very roots of the jumping code – especially if you have a well-stocked picnic hamper in the car.

Bath

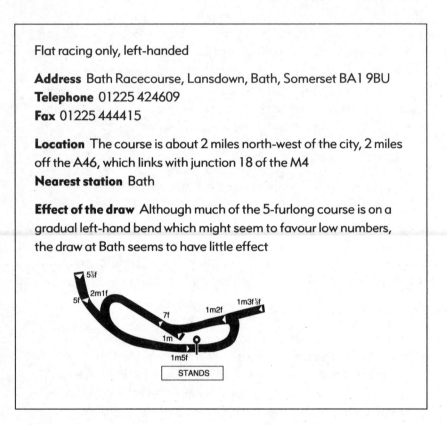
At 780 feet above sea level, Bath is the highest Flat course in the country. Although its location is much loftier than its status – Bath is unarguably in the minor league of Flat tracks – the course is famed for the quality of its downland turf. Over the years it has proved an ideal testing ground for promising two-year-olds before they graduate to the more prestigious tracks.

The circuit is just over a mile and a half round, and although the turns at each end of the track are fairly tight, the course is generally galloping rather than sharp in nature. The run-in from the home turn rises all the way to the winning post, and bends noticeably to the left about two furlongs out, which can cause bunching and puts a premium on skilful jockeyship: it can be rewarding for punters to pay close attention to which riders have done well at Bath over the years.

Bath was the site of a famous coup in 1953 when a horse named Francasal won a seller at 10–1, then turned out to be not Francasal at all but a 'ringer' – a much faster horse named Santa Amaro. Four of the perpetrators of the coup ended up in jail.

A particularly appealing feature of Bath from the spectator's point of view is that, since the shape of the course is that of a squashed sausage, the crowd in the stands has a very close-up view of the action even when the runners are on the far side.

Beverley

Flat racing only, right-handed

Address The Grandstand, York Road, Beverley, East Yorkshire
HU17 8QZ
Telephone 01482 867488
Fax 01482 863892

Location Beverley is about 10 miles north of Hull; the racecourse is
on the western side of the town off the A1035; nearest motorway:
M62, junction 38
Nearest station Beverley, 2 miles from course

Effect of the draw High numbers are significantly favoured in
5-furlong races

There has been horse racing on the Westwood, an area of common
land just outside the cathedral town of Beverley, since 1690, and
today the same land is the site of an unpretentious, well-run
racecourse with a strong local following.

Rapid Lad won twelve races at Beverley between 1983 and 1989.
The course now stages the Rapid Lad Handicap in his honour.

The round course is a right-handed oval just over one mile three
furlongs in circumference, with five-furlong sprints starting from a
chute: runners in five-furlong races negotiate a slight right-hand

bend as that chute meets the round course, and spend most of the race on a steady uphill rise, which means that the trip takes some getting, especially for early-season two-year-olds. The round course is mostly galloping in nature, but there is a downhill run along the back straight and the run-in from the home turn is less than three furlongs, favouring the well-balanced horse.

Brighton

Flat racing only, left-handed

Address Brighton Racecourse, Freshfield Road, Racehill, Brighton, East Sussex BN2 2XZ
Telephone 01273 603580
Fax 01273 673267

Location The racecourse is on the eastern side of the town, off the A259 Brighton–Newhaven road
Nearest station Brighton: courtesy buses to course

Effect of the draw Low numbers favoured in sprint races, but high numbers when the going is soft

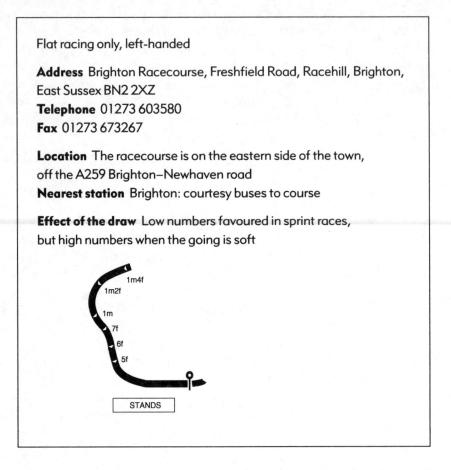

Somehow Brighton racecourse has never quite managed to shrug off the reputation it acquired in Graham Greene's 1938 novel *Brighton Rock* as the stamping ground of razor-toting gangs, but nowadays the chance of bumping into Richard Attenborough on the raceday sponsored by the Labour Party is greater than that of encountering Pinkie, the character he played in the film of the novel. Yet like the town, the racecourse retains a slight air of raffishness.

One of the four tracks in the country which is not a circuit (the others are Epsom Downs, Newmarket and York), the course is in the shape of a hammered-out horseshoe a fraction short of a mile and a half in length. Runners tackling the longest distance raced over here, one mile three furlongs 196 yards (called one and a half miles before the course was properly measured), go uphill from the start for about half a mile, negotiating left-hand turns, then, turning for home about five furlongs out, downhill until a quarter of a mile out, when the ground rises again.

Operatic Society, one of the most popular geldings on the Flat since the war, ran fourteen times at Brighton and won seven races on the course, where there are now a bar and a race named after him.

Uphill and downhill, sweeping left-hand turns – sounds familiar? . . . The terrain of Brighton has distinct similarities with that of the Derby course at Epsom Downs, and time was when Brighton was considered a course on which trainers could assess the agility and balance of their Classic hopefuls. With a series of valuable trials taking place elsewhere, Brighton has lost favour in this respect in recent years, and the last horse to run prominently in the Derby after flexing his muscles around here was Cacoethes, third to Nashwan in 1989: his seasonal debut had been in a minor race at Brighton.

The undulations make Brighton a course for the nimble and quick-actioned rather than the long-striding type of horse.

With much of the action skirting a housing estate, Brighton is not the most scenic track in the country, but it commands wonderful views of the English Channel, and with many of its fixtures catering for large holiday crowds, the atmosphere is usually one of relaxed jollity.

Carlisle

Flat and National Hunt, right-handed

Address Durdar Road, Carlisle, Cumbria CA2 4TS
Telephone 01228 522973
Fax 01228 591827

Location The racecourse is 3 miles south of the town centre,
2 miles from junction 42 of the M6
Nearest station Carlisle, 2 miles from racecourse (bus to course)

Effect of the draw High numbers tend to have an advantage in
distances up to 1 mile

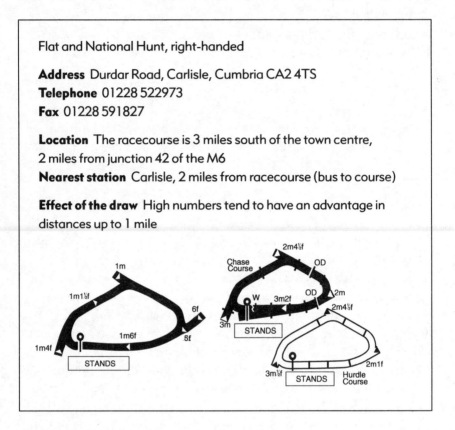

Carlisle is such a roller-coaster of a course that parts of the action down the far side can be viewed only from the upper reaches of the charming but roofless grandstand, erected when the course was established on its present site in the first decade of this century.

The undulations make Carlisle a particularly testing track under both Flat and National Hunt codes, especially when the going gets heavy (as it frequently does during the jumping season).

The sticky toffee pudding sold at Carlisle racecourse is, according to experts, one of the finest foodstuffs to be had in the sporting world.

The circuit is pear-shaped, a little over twelve furlongs round. Beyond the winning post the track sweeps downhill, then rises for a while before levelling out about a mile from home. But the straight involves a steep rise until just before the post, so stamina is always at a premium here.

Red Rum ran in the Windermere Handicap Chase at Carlisle on five occasions, all but once as his seasonal debut. He won the race three times, and finished second and third on the other two occasions.

Cartmel

National Hunt only, left-handed

Address Cartmel Racecourse, Cartmel, Cumbria LA11 6QF
Telephone 01539 536340

Location Cartmel is about 16 miles south-west of Kendal;
access from M6 junction 36
Nearest stations Cark-in-Cartmel or Grange-over-Sands, both
2½ miles from course (bus to course from each)

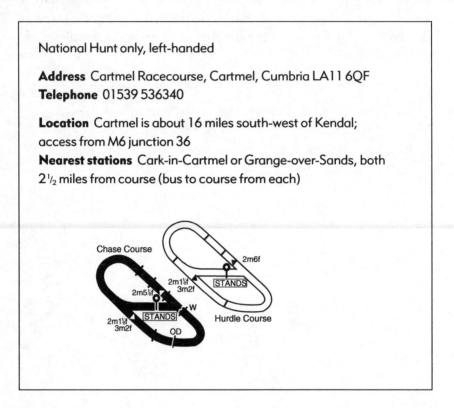

There is nowhere in the racing world like Cartmel. On the edge of a
small Lakeland village otherwise famed for its priory, the course
snuggles up on one side against the stone walls at the end of
delightful cottage gardens, on the other against dense woodland.
The track itself is the shortest and oddest in jump racing, the quality
of the racing is bargain-basement, the facilities are basic in the
extreme (there is no covered grandstand), it is effectively impossible
for any racegoer to get an uninterrupted view of the races themselves
– and yet a day at Cartmel is one of the most wonderful experiences
racing in Britain can offer.

Plenty of people share that opinion, and crowds swarm to
Cartmel in their tens of thousands: on Spring Bank Holiday Monday
1997, for example, a crowd of over 21,000 crammed into the
course. For many of this host, the racing is literally a peripheral

activity. They drive their cars into the infield, spread out their picnics, visit the large funfair which occupies half the course, and generally have a great day out in the open air – one punctuated every half hour by a handful of racehorses whizzing by on the outside of the picnic area. Visitors who venture beyond the funfair come across a sign reading 'BARBECUE AREA' which designates a large field dedicated to that very activity, with hundreds of barbecues spluttering away.

Royal Ascot it ain't.

Cartmel was the venue for the most audacious betting coup of recent years – the Gay Future affair on 26 August 1974, Bank Holiday Monday. The essence of this intricate and ingenious coup was that Gay Future had been extensively backed in doubles and trebles with two other horses in the yard of Scottish trainer Anthony Collins, but the other horses were both withdrawn from their races (in fact they never left Collins's yard that day), transforming all those multiples into singles. The horse in Collins's yard, however, was not actually Gay Future at all. The real Gay Future had been secretly prepared in Ireland by Eddie O'Grady, was shipped over on the Monday morning and swapped with the horse trained by Collins, and bolted in at 10–1. The bookies – unable to lay off when they realised what was going on as there was no 'blower' service to Cartmel and this was well before the days of mobile phones – cried foul and the police were called in, with the result that two of the plotters were eventually convicted of conspiracy to defraud the bookmakers.

The circuit at Cartmel mirrors the quirkiness of the occasion. Little over a mile round, left-handed, mildly undulating and very tight, it demands a compact, nippy sort of horse. Choose such a horse and back him, then hope to catch the odd glimpse of him during the race as he charges past the funfair, past the trees, past the massed crowds. The steeplechase fences are sited very irregularly, and one of Cartmel's most disorientating features is that when the runners take the last fence they are going away from the stand: they have still to come round the final bend and up the chute which forms the finishing straight – at half a mile the longest run-in on any chasing course.

If the horses in action at Cartmel are rarely top-class, the jockeys frequently are. The Dunwoodys and McCoys of this world, who know an opportunity for fun when they see it, are regular visitors.

Tradition has it that racing at Cartmel began in the Middle Ages when the monks at the priory started racing their mules across the sands, and there was organised racing on the present site in the late nineteenth century. For many years Cartmel raced only at its two-day Whitsun meeting; then another two days were added at August Bank Holiday weekend; and in 1997–8 there were just six opportunities to enjoy this jewel among racecourses.

If you don't enjoy racing at Cartmel, give up!

Catterick

Flat and National Hunt, left-handed

Address Catterick Racecourse Company Ltd, Catterick Bridge, Richmond, North Yorkshire DL10 7PE
Telephone 01748 811478
Fax 01748 811082

Location The racecourse is about 10 miles south of Darlington and 1 mile north-west of Catterick, adjacent to the A1
Nearest station Darlington (bus service to course)

Effect of the draw Over 5 furlongs, low numbers favoured except when the ground is soft, when high numbers favoured; over 6 and 7 furlongs, low numbers favoured as long as the horse is not a slow starter

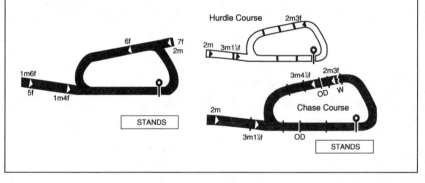

The Flat circuit at Catterick is just under nine furlongs round, undulating and with tight bends – tailor-made for the nippy starter with a catch-me-if-you-can approach; there is never much time to make up lost ground before the next bend, and the course's sharpness militates against the big, long-striding sort of horse. The five-furlong course starts with a downhill stretch and is very fast.

The jumping circuit is longer than the Flat at about one and a quarter miles, and down the back straight runs parallel with but completely detached from the Flat course. But as with the Flat, the course does not favour the galloping type of horse but rather the nifty sort who can set off sharply. The speed at which jumpers tear round Catterick makes this an awkward place for a novice chaser – if you're tempted to bet in a novice chase here, make sure your selection comes from a yard which is known for schooling its young horses well.

Racing was staged at Catterick as long ago as the seventeenth century, with regular fixtures on the site of the present course dating back to 1783. Facilities at the course had a major boost with the opening of a new grandstand in July 1998.

Gods Solution, owned by Peter Jones (now chairman of the Tote), won the same six-furlong handicap at Catterick's early-season meeting six times: 1985–9 and 1991. In 1990 the race was renamed the Gods Solution Handicap in his honour, but he could finish only third. The following year, as a ten-year-old, Gods Solution picked up the winning thread in the race for his eighth course win and was promptly retired. A bar in the new grandstand commemorates his Catterick achievements.

While Catterick may not be the obvious place to spot future Classic winners, do not despair of ever seeing a top-class horse here: Opale, winner of the 1984 Irish St Leger, opened her career with a victory in a maiden race at Catterick in June 1983: she started at 50–1!

Tommo's tip . . .
'It always pays here to follow two-year-olds trained by Jack Berry.'

Cheltenham

National Hunt only, left-handed

Address Cheltenham
Racecourse, Prestbury Park,
Cheltenham, Gloucestershire
GL50 4SH
Telephone 01242 513014 (for
bookings: 01242 226226)
Fax 01242 224227
E-mail admin@
cheltenhamracecourse.co.uk
Web www.cheltenham.co.uk

Location The racecourse is 1½ miles north of the town on the
A435; access from M5 junctions 10 or 11
Nearest station Cheltenham Spa, 2 miles from racecourse (bus
to course)

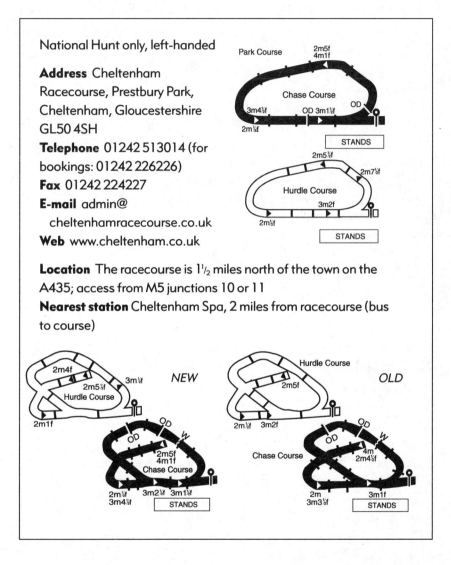

Set in glorious Cotswold countryside, with Cleeve Hill looming at the
far end of the course to form a natural backdrop, Cheltenham is the
spiritual home of National Hunt racing. The entire jumping season is
dominated by and geared towards one meeting here, the National
Hunt Festival in March: three days of the very best steeplechasing and
hurdling (and one National Hunt Flat race), top horses, vast crowds,

hordes of Irish visitors, huge excitement. No wonder the ailing Irishman, when told by his doctor that he had three days to live, asked if those three days could be at Cheltenham in mid-March . . .

Unlike many other great sporting jamborees, the Cheltenham Festival we know today is the result of evolution rather than careful planning, and its shape is still being subtly altered: the 'bumper', for example – the National Hunt Flat race which closes the programme on the second day – has been run only since 1992.

Highlight of the first day – Tuesday – is the Champion Hurdle over an extended two miles, the undisputed championship event for the best hurdlers. Since the war it has been won by all the greats – including three-times winners Hatton's Grace, Sir Ken, Persian War and See You Then, and dual scorers National Spirit, Bula, Comedy Of Errors, Night Nurse, Monksfield and Sea Pigeon.

Channel Four Racing have been covering Cheltenham since the beginning of 1995.

Wednesday features the Queen Mother Champion Chase over two miles for the cream of the chasing speed merchants. The sight of the field thundering down the hill and swinging round the home turn to face the final fence is one of the great experiences for jumping fans, who have been rewarded in recent years with some wonderful races featuring such individuals as Badsworth Boy (the only horse to win the race three times) and dual winners Pearlyman, Barnbrook Again and the massively popular Viking Flagship, as well as the likes of Buck House, Remittance Man and Martha's Son. The brilliant grey One Man raised the Cheltenham roof when winning this race in March 1998 to eradicate grim memories of his two failures in the Gold Cup, but the race proved to be his last victory: sixteen days later he was killed at Aintree.

Thursday is Gold Cup day itself, with a crowd of over fifty thousand squeezing into the course to produce an atmosphere unlike any other occasion in racing. The Gold Cup is run over three and a quarter miles – two and a bit circuits of the course – and stands unassailed as the true championship of staying steeplechasers, its list of winners a roll-call of the giants: Golden Miller five times, Arkle and Cottage Rake three times, Easter Hero and L'Escargot twice, Prince Regent, Mandarin, Mill House, The Dikler, Captain Christy, Burrough Hill Lad, Dawn Run (the only horse ever to win Champion Hurdle and Gold Cup) and Desert Orchid. It is a race whose history brims with stories: the extraordinary feat of Michael Dickinson training the first five home in 1983; the 100–1 victory in 1990 of Norton's Coin, trained by a dairy farmer; justice asserting itself when The Fellow, twice short-headed in the race, finally kept his nose in front in 1994; or the manic scenes of Irish celebration greeting Dawn Run in 1986 and Imperial Call ten years later.

As with Royal Ascot on the Flat, the strength of the National Hunt Festival is its depth, and the three peaks are supported by a host of other major races:

- three big races for novice hurdlers: the Triumph Hurdle (two miles), top four-year-old hurdle of the season; the Supreme Novices' Hurdle (two miles); and the Royal & SunAlliance Novices' Hurdle (two miles five furlongs);
- major novice chases in the shape of the Arkle Trophy (two miles) and the Royal & SunAlliance Novices' Chase (three miles one furlong);
- the Stayers' Hurdle (three miles) and the Vincent O'Brien County Hurdle (two miles one furlong);
- more big steeplechases in the National Hunt Chase (three miles one furlong), the Mildmay of Flete Challenge Cup (two and a half miles), the Cathcart Challenge Cup (two miles five furlongs) and the Foxhunter Chase (three and a quarter miles).

For sheer atmosphere unadulterated by any concerns of fashion, there is simply no race meeting to compare with the Cheltenham Festival. True, some fainthearts complain that the crush is too much, that it takes too long to queue for a drink, that it's too much of an effort to get out of the car park after racing, and that the smell of fried onions from the burger bars is just *too* pervasive – but everyone else comes determined to enjoy themselves, and few go home having failed to do that.

The rest of the Cheltenham year is pretty good as well. In November the course stages the Murphy's Gold Cup – previously the Mackeson – a steeplechase over an extended two and a half miles which marks the effective beginning of the serious core of the jumping season. The same meeting sees the Sporting Index Chase over three miles seven furlongs of the cross-country course built in the infield of the main track and first used in 1995: purists shake their heads at the sight of stay-for-ever chasers belting round this curious circuit of natural hedges, banks and timber – a sort of mongrel bred from the La Touche Cup course at Punchestown and the Velka Pardubicka track in the Czech Republic – but McGregor The Third has no complaints: he proved the easy winner of the first two runnings.

The December meeting has the Tripleprint Gold Cup over two miles five furlongs, companion race to the Murphy's Gold Cup; this event began life in 1963 as the Massey-Ferguson Gold Cup and under various names has been won by horses of the quality of Flyingbolt, Pendil and Dublin Flyer. Pegwell Bay and the dashing grey Senor El Betrutti are the only horses to have won the November and December highlights in the same year. The December meeting also features the Bula Hurdle, named after the great Champion Hurdler trained by Fred Winter.

The pre-Festival meeting at the end of January is regularly used by Gold Cup aspirants for a dress rehearsal: for example, Master Oats took the Pillar Chase here in 1995 en route to his moment of glory in March.

Of the twenty-five Grade One races scheduled for the 1997–8 season, eleven were run at Cheltenham – ten at the Festival.

There are three distinct circuits at Cheltenham. Racing switches between the Old Course and the New Course through the season so that the ground is given time to recover from each meeting, and the characteristics of both are broadly the same: a left-handed oval about one and a half miles round, with long straights and no sharp bends. From the stands the runners sweep left and head out into the country, turning at the far end of that straight to negotiate a stiff uphill climb, from the peak of which they sweep sharply downhill – fences on this stretch are particularly problematic – before making the turn towards home. (That downhill stretch is farther from the stands on the New Course, which is slightly longer than the Old.) Two fences are jumped in the straight on the New Course, just one on the Old, but from the last on either circuit the run to the winning post is an exceptionally tough uphill haul, and the complexion of many a Cheltenham race has changed on the run-in as tired horses meet that rising ground.

In addition, there is an extension which bisects the downhill stretch of the main courses, and in 1991 this extension was joined to the New Course to form a circuit known as the Park Course, used at early-season meetings and a less demanding proposition for horses than having to slog all the way to the top of the hill.

Cheltenham racecourse has a marriage licence and can be used for civil wedding ceremonies.

Both the main courses are very testing in their nature, with well-built fences putting a premium on jumping ability for chasers and the fierce uphill finish really plumbing the depths of a horse's resolution and stamina. So while Cheltenham is suited to a galloping type of horse (so long as it can gallop both uphill and downhill), its undulations are not to all tastes, and horses who do well on a flatter surface are sometimes uncomfortable here.

As befits the prestige venue of the sport, jockeyship is of paramount importance at Cheltenham, and experience of how to ride the last mile here – in particular, how to keep momentum over those downhill fences without risking a fall – can prove invaluable.

The opening of the new Tattersalls grandstand in 1997 marked another stage in an extensive development programme which has seen major changes over the years: the parade ring, for example, is now a prominent feature of the Cheltenham racegoing experience, as the paddock incorporates the winner's enclosure (a layout followed at several other courses) and the winner returns to face his or her adoring public massed on the terraces.

Brough Scott's favourite . . .

'Cheltenham was the first racecourse I can ever remember going to, and it was at Frenchie Nicholson's yard next to the course that I first got the bug for racing. To have ridden at Cheltenham, and now to have the privilege of presenting Channel Four Racing from there, is a central part of my racing dream.'

. . . and Alastair Down's favourite . . .

'It is races rather than places that grip me, but the abiding exception to that remains Cheltenham. Even in high summer, the mind is drawn to it like an old and valued friend whom you don't need to see every five minutes in order to maintain the bond. It is a place of endeavour, emotion and occasionally sadness. But I have witnessed dramas played out there that will stay forever young in the mind long after other memories have succumbed to sepia.'

Cheltenham may be looking to the future, but it has due respect for the past. Statues of Arkle, Golden Miller and Dawn Run face the parade ring. The Arkle Bar, a traditional meeting place, is not just another racecourse bar named after a great horse but almost a museum, with plenty of cuttings and souvenirs recalling the greatest career of all – including those famous envelopes addressed to 'Arkle, Ireland'. And no visit is complete without a decent spell in the Hall of Fame, an extensive and very well-mounted exhibition of the feats of the horses and people who have made Cheltenham the shrine it is today.

Although a permanent course was laid out at the current site in 1902, there had been racing at Prestbury, the adjacent village, as far back as 1831: the Grand Annual Steeplechase, still an event on the Festival programme, was run there in 1834. The first Gold Cup was run in 1924, the inaugural Champion Hurdle three years later.

Opposite: Coming into the home straight at Kempton Park.

Midsummer highlights at *(above)* Royal Ascot and *(below)* Glorious Goodwood.

Big occasions at jumping tracks great and small. *Above:* The National Hunt Festival at Cheltenham; *below:* Spring Bank Holiday at Cartmel.

Classic courses. *Above:* At Epsom Downs, Sunshine Street leads the
1998 Vodafone Derby field round Tattenham Corner; *below:* Doncaster,
home of the St Leger. *Opposite above:* The Rowley Mile at Newmarket,
home of the Two Thousand Guineas and One Thousand Guineas.

The July Course at Newmarket.

Above: Loading up at Chester; *below:* The winner's enclosure at York, with the Terry's chocolate factory in the background.

Above: Sandown Park in all its glory, with Desert Orchid halfway to winning the 1988 Whitbread Gold Cup; *below:* Jumping the last at Warwick.

Home turns. *Above:* Splashing about on the all-weather surface
at Southwell; *below:* Swinging into the straight at Newbury.

Chepstow

Flat and National Hunt, left-handed

Address Chepstow Racecourse, Chepstow, Gwent NP6 5YH
Telephone 01291 622260
Fax 01291 625550
Web www.chepstow-racecourse.co.uk

Location The racecourse is 1 mile north-west of the town of
Chepstow on the A466, easily accessible from the M4 junction 22
Nearest station Chepstow, 1½ miles from racecourse (bus to
course)

Effect of the draw No marked advantage either side

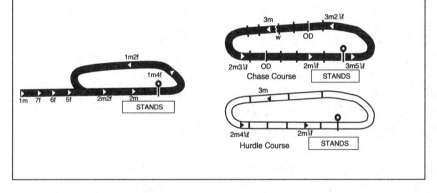

Chepstow is one of the more modern courses in Britain, having been
opened in 1926 – although there has been racing in the locality since
the eighteenth century.

At just short of two miles round, the circuit is tailor-made for the
doughty stayer. Its back straight and home straight are each long
enough to tax the determination and stamina of even the stoutest
horse, but it is extremely undulating, and thus not ideal for the long-
striding galloper.

On the Flat, there is a straight mile, and all distances shorter than
one mile are run on the straight course. But it is as a jumping track
that Chepstow really excels, and never more so than when it stages

one of the very big races – and best racegoing occasions – of the jumping year: the Welsh National just after Christmas. The race starts right in front of the stands and takes in two complete circuits of the course to make its trip of three miles five and a half furlongs a true test of stamina – notably up the home straight, where there are five fences to be jumped. The Welsh National has seen some gargantuan achievements in recent times, none more so than that of Carvill's Hill, who ground his rivals into the mud in 1991 with one of the most relentless front-running performances in memory. Two winners in the last fifteen years have gone on from Chepstow to win the Cheltenham Gold Cup – Burrough Hill Lad (1983) in the same season and 1990 winner Cool Ground in 1992 – while 1997 winner Earth Summit landed the Grand National later the same season: if a horse can stay three and three-quarter miles round Chepstow, four and a half round the flat surface of Aintree should be a doddle.

On 4 October 1933 Gordon Richards rode the winners of all six races at Chepstow, then the winners of the first five races at the course the following day. In the sixth he was beaten on 3–1 on shot Eagle Ray.

Chepstow hosts several other significant National Hunt races. The Rehearsal Chase in early December is a valuable opportunity for staying chasers to warm up for the King George at Kempton (1997 winner See More Business duly did the double); the Persian War Novices' Hurdle in February commemorates the triple Champion Hurdle winner; the John Hughes Grand National Trial in February provides pointers to the Aintree marathon; and in April the Welsh Champion Hurdle is often a consolation prize for horses who have missed out in the 'real' championship at Cheltenham the previous month.

Chester

Flat racing only, left-handed

Address Chester Racecourse, Chester, Cheshire CH1 2LY
Telephone 01244 323170
Fax 01244 344971

Location The racecourse is close to the centre of the city, on the A548
Nearest station Chester, 1 mile from racecourse (bus to course)

Effect of the draw Low numbers tend to be favoured, but the all-important factor is a quick break, whatever the draw

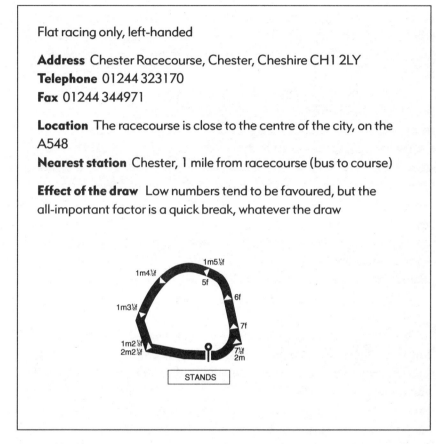

Chester is such an extraordinary racecourse that no description can do it justice. But we'll try anyway . . .

The track is an oval – not far off a circle – a few yards over one mile round, which makes this the shortest Flat course in the country. About half the circuit is bordered by the River Dee; the short straight after the winning post runs parallel to the railway line; and the stands and home straight nestle up against the city's old Roman walls, from which skint racing fans and casual passers-by can enjoy a wonderful view of the sport for free.

The surface is completely flat, runners are never far from the next turn, and the home straight is under two furlongs long. So good jockeyship can be crucial at Chester: punters do well to follow pilots who have proved that they have mastered its curiosities.

The May Meeting – the course's and the city's great annual event – is noted for its Classic trials: the Chester Vase (one and a half miles), Cheshire Oaks (one mile three furlongs) and Dee Stakes (one and a quarter miles). Chester, like Epsom, requires nimbleness and balance in a racehorse, and it is no coincidence that horses which act well here can go on to greater things at the Surrey course. In 1959 Parthia won the Dee Stakes before landing the Derby, but the Chester Vase tends to be a stronger race: in recent years Henbit and Shergar both won this before going on to Epsom success, and other notable winners since then have been Law Society, Unfuwain, Old Vic and Belmez; Quest For Fame, second to Belmez in 1990, won that year's Derby.

Chester is popularly known as the Roodeye or Roodee – from an old phrase meaning the meadow ('eye') of the cross ('rood'). A stone cross, the pedestal of which remains, stood on the site.

For all those dreams of Classics, the big race of the May Meeting – and thus of the Chester year – is the Chester Cup over two and a quarter miles, which amounts to two and a quarter circuits of the track, passing the winning post three times. You'd think such a test would make any horse dizzy, but the race has been won by some famous stayers, including Brown Jack, Trelawny, Attivo (owned by Peter O'Sullevan), John Cherry and Sea Pigeon, who won the race twice – a feat repeated in 1995 and 1997 by Top Cees.

The other big race of the May Meeting is the Ormonde Stakes over one mile five furlongs, which since the war has been won by three Derby winners: Tulyar before his Epsom victory in 1952 and Blakeney (1970) and Teenoso (1984) as four-year-olds.

Chester racecourse is the oldest horse racing venue in Britain: there were races here early in the reign of Henry VIII, and the Silver Bell run for at the invitation of the mayor on Shrove Tuesday 1540 was the first recorded regular prize.

Given the tightness of the area available, space is at a premium at Chester, and the parade ring and weighing room are inside the track:

racegoers have access from the stands by means of a tunnel. The old County Stand was severely damaged by fire in 1985 and replaced in 1988 by a new building, but there are enough parts of the older enclosures left to give a wonderful period feel – and the course is so close to the centre of the city that after a successful day you can miss the last and nip up to the excellent shops to redistribute your winnings.

John McCririck's favourite . . .

'No racecourse can ever replace the late lamented Alexandra Park in my affections, but Chester comes close. The history of the place, the crowds, the intimacy – a great place to come racing. And a key part of its appeal is that the parade ring is in front of the stands. At Chester – and at those other enterprising courses where the paddock is similarly placed – you can get close to the horses paddock-side if you want, or you can stay in the stand and still see what's going on. When you go to see a play you don't have to go scurrying round behind the theatre for each new bit of the action: each new scene is brought to you. Why can't more racecourses follow that example?'

Doncaster

Flat and National Hunt, left-handed

Address Doncaster Racecourse, The Grandstand, Leger Way, Doncaster, South Yorkshire DN2 6BB
Telephone 01302 320066
Fax 01302 323271

Location The racecourse is on the eastern side of the town, at the junction of the A18 and A638; access from M18 junctions 3 or 4
Nearest station Doncaster, 2 miles from racecourse (bus to course)

Effect of the draw Low numbers used to be favoured in big fields on the straight course when the going is soft, but the effect is becoming increasingly difficult to predict

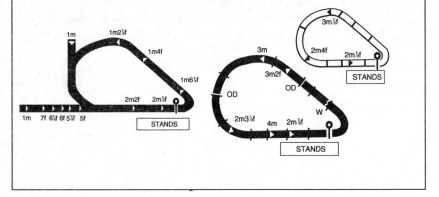

Home of the St Leger, first run in 1776 and oldest of the Classics, Doncaster is a racecourse steeped in history. There were races run on the Town Moor – where the course is still situated, though the first two St Legers were run on the adjacent Cantley Common – in the late sixteenth century, and ever since then the sport has been an important facet of Doncaster life: today the St Leger fixture is the northern equivalent of Derby Day, with a large funfair dispensing jollity alongside the racetrack, a huge crowd and general air of merriment.

The St Leger may not be quite the race it once was – though the clamour for it to be opened to horses older than three seems to have died down – and Donny itself has had spells in the doldrums, but the course underwent a complete facelift in 1969, with the parade ring re-sited directly in front of a vast new grandstand. The indoor betting hall which formed part of that stand proved unpopular – punter versus bookmaker is an elemental struggle between conflicting forces of nature which must be conducted in the open air – and after a while the layers returned to the great outdoors.

Doncaster is acknowledged to be one of the fairest and best racing surfaces in the country. The circuit is left-handed and pear-shaped, a little under two miles round, with the 'sharp end' of the pear after the winning post providing the only tight bend; the other turn is a very long, sweeping curve which need cause no interruption to the rhythm of a galloping horse. The only significant undulation on the circuit is a small rise and fall – Rose Hill – about ten furlongs out, and the run from the home turn up the wide straight is just under five furlongs. Thus Doncaster is the ideal venue for the long-striding galloper, a place where a horse needs to see out every yard of the trip.

The Doncaster Cup is one of the oldest races still run under Rules: first contested in 1766, it pre-dates all of the Classics.

The jumping course has in its time been criticised for the perceived easiness of the steeplechase fences; like the Flat track, it is a place for the galloping rather than the nippy type of animal. From the last fence to the winning post is a little over one furlong.

Doncaster provides the book-ends of the Flat season proper. All-weather racing may have been on the go since the very beginning of the year, but it is the first turf fixture at Donny in late March that heralds the traditional 'Start of the Flat'. That meeting features the Lincoln Handicap, one of the big betting races of the year, with a large field hammering up the straight mile. At the other end of the season, the November meeting with the November Handicap (one and a half miles) marks the close of the Flat on turf.

But Doncaster's greatest race, and greatest occasion, is unarguably the St Leger. Run over one mile six furlongs 132 yards in mid-September, the final Classic has in the last twenty years or so seen off the critics to resume its place as one of the landmarks of the racing year. Leger Day racegoers like nothing more than to see the race bring up a Classic double (or even treble), and they have in recent years given rousing ovations to the Queen's Dunfermline, who beat Alleged after a titanic struggle in 1977 to add the Leger to her Oaks, and to Sun Princess (Oaks and St Leger 1983), Oh So Sharp (One Thousand Guineas, Oaks and St Leger – the 'Fillies' Triple Crown' – in 1985) and Reference Point (Derby and St Leger 1987).

The St Leger is the high point of the four-day September meeting which also features the Champagne Stakes over seven furlongs and the Flying Childers Stakes over five furlongs, both for two-year-olds. The May Hill Stakes over the round mile is a Group Three event for staying two-year-old fillies, and older fillies have a Group Three race over the full St Leger distance in the Park Hill Stakes. The Doncaster Cup over two and a quarter miles is the final leg of the 'Stayers' Triple Crown', following on from the Ascot Gold Cup and the Goodwood Cup. The last horse to complete that notable treble was Double Trigger in 1995.

· Frankie Dettori's victory on Classic Cliche in the 1995 Pertemps St Leger was the 1,000th victory of his riding career in Britain. Pat Eddery's win on Silver Patriarch in the 1997 St Leger was his 4,000th victory in Britain.

Doncaster's other Group One event, apart from the St Leger, is the Racing Post Trophy over the round mile in October. This race – the only Group One two-year-old contest over a mile and the last Group One of the season in Britain – started life as the Timeform Gold Cup back in 1961, and under its various guises has produced winners of the calibre of Noblesse, Ribocco, Vaguely Noble, High Top, Reference Point (the only winner of the race to go on and land the Derby the following year), King's Theatre and Celtic Swing.

Jumping at Doncaster does not seem to enjoy the status it did when the Great Yorkshire Chase was one of the big races of the season, but the overall standard of sport is good. The Great Yorkshire is run in January and remains a competitive handicap chase over three miles, even if it lacks the cachet of the days when it was a natural step on the way to the Grand National.

Epsom Downs

Flat racing only, left-handed

Address Epsom Downs, Epsom, Surrey KT18 5LQ
Telephone 01372 726311
Fax 01372 748253

Location Epsom Downs is 2 miles south of the town of Epsom on the B390, 5 miles from the M25 (junction 8 or 9)
Nearest station Tattenham Corner (from London Bridge, Charing Cross, Victoria or Waterloo), 15 minutes' walk from grandstand

Effect of the draw High numbers strongly favoured over 5 furlongs, slightly favoured over 6

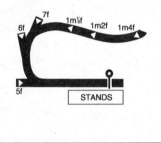

Epsom Downs, home of the Derby and Oaks, is one of the most historic racecourses in the country – and that history is inextricably linked with the town above which the racecourse perches, affording modern racegoers spectacular views of London.

By the middle of the seventeenth century Epsom had become one of the most frequented spa towns in England, its waters notable for their purgative effect. The fame of the Epsom waters (and the Epsom salts which were produced from them) spread far and wide – Samuel Pepys in 1667 drank four pints of the water 'and had some very good stools by it' – and as the town became a magnet for those craving the medicinal properties of the area, so horse races on the Downs became part of local social activity.

Although Epsom's status as a spa town declined during the eighteenth century, racing on the Downs continued. The first running of the Oaks took place in 1779, with the inaugural Derby on 4 May the following year.

That 1780 race was a far cry from today's familiar event, with its climb up the hill, helter-skelter charge down to Tattenham Corner and the final surge up the straight: the first Derby was run over a dog-leg course of just one mile (the distance of the race was not increased to a mile and a half until 1784), starting to the east of the present Tattenham Corner.

'The Derby is a little like your first experience of sex – hectic, strenuous, memorably pleasant and over before you know it' – *Bill Bryson*

The present Derby course, which has been used for the race since 1872, starts opposite the stands. After leaving the stalls the field gets into its stride over a short uphill run into a gradual right-hand bend, then shifts across to the opposite running rail and continues towards the top of Tattenham Hill, 502 feet above sea level. From there the runners engage a sweeping left-handed descent into Tattenham Corner, where, a little under four furlongs from the winning post, they swing into the straight. After that hectic charge downhill, the danger of swinging too wide is very real: in the 1972 Derby the French colt Lyphard, joint second favourite, blew his chance when doing just that, causing journalist Roger Mortimer to observe that jockey Freddie Head 'was unable to control Lyphard who went so wide that he appeared desirous of visiting relatives in Putney'.

The gradient in the straight is a gradual downwards incline until the ground levels out and rises slightly just before the winning post. But that home straight poses a particularly trappy problem for the tired young horse trying to get home: its camber. The ground slopes down from the stands side towards the infield, causing tired horses to hang to their left.

The course has long been the subject of debate: do its ups and downs, its right- and left-hand bends, provide the ultimate test of the athleticism of the Thoroughbred racehorse, or is Epsom a crazy terrain over which to stage serious horse racing? Australian jockey Mick Goreham, who rode in the 1974 Derby, had forthright views:

'It's the queerest course I've ever ridden on. It's not just the hill but the angle. I never expected to see anything like that. And to think you run the greatest race in the world on it. I feel most trainers back home would take one look at it and put their horses right back in the box!'

Although Epsom's three major races – Derby, Oaks and Coronation Cup – are all run over that mile and a half, the course also supplies distances of five, six and seven furlongs, one mile and half a furlong, and one and a quarter miles. Races over six and seven furlongs start from spurs off the round course, while the straight five furlongs starting beyond Tattenham Corner provides the fastest sprint track in the world. It was in the Tadworth Handicap over this course in 1960 that Indigenous, carrying nine stone five pounds and ridden by Lester Piggott, established the fastest ever time for five furlongs – 53.6 seconds.

Over any distance, the key requirement of an Epsom horse is balance, the ability to stay on an even keel over the course's unusual contours. But over the Classic distance that sense of equilibrium must be complemented by adaptability. The ideal Derby or Oaks horse has the speed to take up and hold a position in the early stages of the race, the agility to go uphill and then steeply downhill and, when the strain of the closing stages begins to bite, the fortitude to keep going up that cambered straight.

The Queen's Stand at Epsom was used by the makers of the James Bond movie *Goldeneye* in 1995 as a location shoot: the building played a Russian airport.

For an expert summary of what makes a Derby horse, who better to ask than the jockey who won the race nine times? Lester Piggott wrote in his autobiography: 'My view of the ideal Derby horse has always been that size is less important than manner of racing. You need a horse that can lay up handy, a few places behind the leaders: getting too far back at Epsom can be disastrous, as there is no part of the course where you can readily make up ground forfeited early on. You have to get into a reasonable place and keep out of trouble as beaten horses fall back on the downhill run towards Tattenham Corner.'

Although the terrain itself retains its historic contours, the facilities at Epsom have undergone significant changes in recent years. A new parade ring has been laid out immediately behind the Queen's Stand, which was opened in 1992 as a state-of-the-art facility, and the mammoth old grandstand has – not before time – undergone extensive refurbishment.

Derby Day is Epsom's greatest occasion by a distance. It may be a far cry from the jamboree the Victorians knew, when the running of the Derby annually triggered an unofficial public holiday, when half of London poured out of the city to revel on the Downs and when Charles Dickens could rhapsodise about how 'On Derby Day, a population rolls and surges and scrambles through the place that may be counted in millions', but it is still a very special day. Huge numbers of racegoers make their way to Epsom Downs – many of them in the open-topped buses which line the inside rail in the straight, tens of thousands to picnic on the hill or spend the afternoon at the funfair, and a select few arrayed in morning dress to hob-nob in the Queen's Stand.

The other big Epsom occasion is Oaks Day, which since 1995 has been on the Friday, the eve of Derby Day. As well as the Oaks, the fillies' equivalent of the Derby, this programme includes the Coronation Cup: for four-year-olds and upwards over the Derby course, this is the first of the big international middle-distance events of the summer and always attracts a small but highly select field.

The Epsom Spring Meeting, revived in 1997 after several years in the fixture-list wilderness, includes the Blue Riband Trial, a useful opportunity for Derby candidates to try out their abilities over the full course, and the Great Metropolitan and the City and Suburban, both handicaps now a shadow of their former distinguished selves. Evening racing has become very popular at Epsom Downs, and the August Bank Holiday Monday fixture includes the Moët and Chandon Silver Magnum – the 'Amateurs' Derby' for gentleman riders over the full Classic distance – which was first run in 1960 and was won four times by John Oaksey.

Exeter

National Hunt only, right-handed

Address Exeter Racecourse, Kennford, near Exeter, Devon
EX6 7XS
Telephone 01392 832599
Fax 01392 833454

Location The racecourse is about 8 miles south of the centre
of Exeter on the A38 (Exeter–Plymouth road), 5 miles from the
southern end of the M5
Nearest station Exeter St Davids, 10 miles from racecourse
(bus to course)

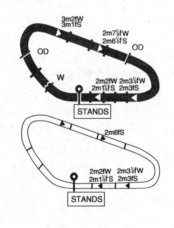

Named 'Devon and Exeter' until dropping the redundant first two
words in 1992, Exeter is an unassuming, friendly little track highly
popular with summertime holidaymakers in the West Country.

The right-handed course, nearly two miles round, undulates
severely – so severely that a stretch at the beginning of the far
straight is obscured from the view of most observers in the stands.
The fences are held to be fairly stiff, and the run from the home turn
is an uphill half mile. So you need a horse here who has plenty of
balance to cope with the undulations, and who won't shirk the issue

in the closing stages. (The winter course uses the outside portion of the track and is thus slightly longer than the summer course: differences in distance are marked 'W' and 'S' on the plans opposite.) You might find the odd winner by considering the course's characteristics, but a much simpler approach to backing Exeter winners is blindly to follow anything trained by Martin Pipe, whose tally of winners here is light years ahead of any other trainer's. No Pipe horse running here offers any value in the betting ring, but better an odds-on winner than a decent-priced loser . . .

On Sunday 28 June 1998 Exeter became the first British racecourse to provide betting facilities for 'away' meetings at Doncaster, Goodwood, Uttoxeter and The Curragh even though there was no racing on the course itself.

Exeter prides itself on being one of the oldest courses in the country: there are records of meetings nearby as long ago as 1738, and evidence exists that there was racing here in the early seventeenth century. Nowadays the sport is fairly modest, but the course can boast one very high-class early-season steeplechase in the Plymouth Gin Haldon Gold Cup, run in early November over two miles one and a half furlongs; winners include Panto Prince, Sabin Du Loir (who won the race twice), Waterloo Boy and Viking Flagship.

Fakenham

National Hunt only, left-handed

Address The Racecourse, Fakenham, Norfolk NR21 7NY
Telephone 01328 862388
Fax 01328 855908

Location Fakenham is 25 miles north-west of Norwich, and the racecourse is 1 mile south of the town on the B1146
Nearest stations King's Lynn (22 miles from the course) or Norwich (25 miles)

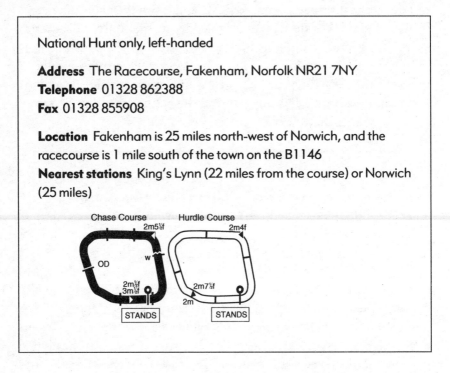

Fakenham is the modern name for the racecourse known until 1963 as the West Norfolk Hunt, which attests to the course's status as one of those hunt-based minor tracks which provide so much of the appeal of British jump racing.

A left-handed square-shaped track of about one mile round, Fakenham is very much a course for front-runners and for the nifty, compact horses who need to take their chances where their long-striding rivals are less comfortable. The short circuit and the tightness of the bends mean that fields tend to go very fast here, and the undulations further militate against the galloping type of horse.

Going racing at Fakenham is an experience not dissimilar from going to a point-to-point: a certain informality, strong connections with the surrounding community and a crowd drawn very much from the locality. The racing will not be top-class, but nobody minds, and there is always a very convivial atmosphere.

Folkestone

Flat and National Hunt, right-handed

Address Folkestone Racecourse, Westenhanger, Hythe, Kent
CT21 4HY
Telephone 01303 266407
Fax 01303 260185

Location Folkestone racecourse is about 5 miles west of the town,
with easy access from the M20 (junction 11)
Nearest station Westenhanger (200 yards from the course)

Effect of the draw High numbers favoured in sprint races

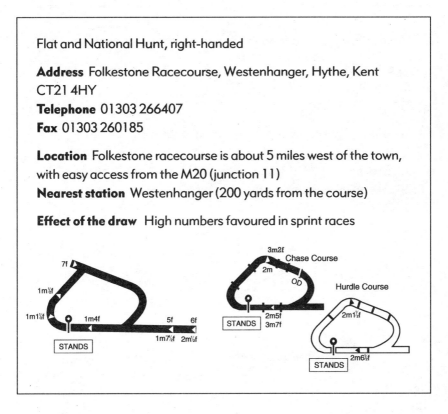

Although not universally popular with all racing professionals (its
sharp nature and less than state-of-the-art facilities are uncongenial
to some trainers and jockeys), Folkestone has its charms, including
its very own goldfish pond – a tranquil spot by which to contemplate
losses.

The only racecourse in Kent since the closure of Wye in 1974, the
current course has staged racing since 1898.

About one mile and three furlongs round and fairly undulating,
the circuit here is tight, and with a home straight of just two and a
half furlongs, it is no place for a horse to lay too far off the pace.
Accordingly it favours the handy, sharp type rather than the resolute
galloper.

Fontwell Park

National Hunt only: left-handed (hurdles); figure-of-eight (chases)

Address Fontwell Park Racecourse, Fontwell, near Arundel, West Sussex BN18 0SX
Telephone 01243 543335

Location Fontwell is 6 miles west of Chichester and 6 miles north of Bognor Regis; the racecourse is south of the village at the junction of the A27 (Brighton–Chichester road) and A29
Nearest station Barnham (London Victoria–Portsmouth line), 2 miles from course

The steeplechase track at Fontwell Park – where racing has taken place since 1924 – is one of Britain's two figure-of-eight courses (the other is Windsor), with all the fences on the criss-cross diagonals; the hurdle course, just over one mile round, forms an oval outside the chase track. Hence your ideal Fontwell horse will be compact, handy, and – especially in the case of chasers – not prone to bouts of dizziness from being so often on the turn. Its peculiarities make it an excellent venue at which to apply the 'horses for courses' theory (see page 16), though any Fontwell specialist these days will have to go some to beat the record of the chaser Certain Justice, who won fourteen races on this track, the last in 1965.

Although the standard of sport here does not rival that at Cheltenham or Sandown Park, Fontwell is a delightful place to go racing, with good facilities and excellent viewing. The key spot for those wishing to experience steeplechasing in the raw is at the central angle of the figure-of-eight, where you can revel in intimate views of several fences and still nip back up the hill for a close-up of the finish. But if the twists and turns of a chase here are confusing to spectators, think what it can be like for a jockey. It's not unusual for even a leading rider to lose count of how many times the field has gone round, and many a pilot has ridden a finish one circuit too early.

It was at Fontwell Park that the Queen – then Princess Elizabeth – had her first winner as an owner: Monaveen in the Chichester Handicap Chase on 10 October 1949. She owned the horse jointly with her mother.

A particular feature of the stands area at Fontwell is the little classical garden tucked away beyond the winning post, a real haven of tranquillity complete with rotunda bearing an inscription in stained glass: 'Be ye therefore followers of God as dear children'. Not many racecourses can claim such closeness to the Almighty.

Goodwood

Flat racing only, right-handed (races over longer distances include left-hand turns)

Address Goodwood Racecourse, Goodwood, Chichester, West Sussex PO18 0PS
Telephone 01243 755022
Fax 01243 755025
E-mail 100270.1141@compuserve.com
Web www.gloriousgoodwood.co.uk

Location Goodwood is 4 miles north of Chichester between the A286 (Midhurst road) and A285 (Petworth road); access from the A27
Nearest station Chichester (Brighton–Portsmouth line), 4 miles from racecourse (bus to course)

Effect of the draw Minimal (under normal circumstances)

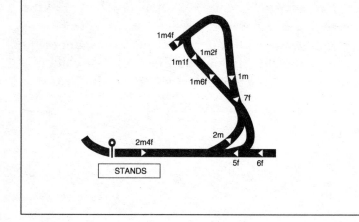

'Glorious Goodwood' – any visitor to this spectacularly sited racecourse high on the Sussex Downs can instantly appreciate the accuracy of that epithet. Although the 'Glorious' tag originally applied to the course's flagship fixture, the July Meeting, the setting is so remarkable, with magnificent views across the surrounding countryside and down to the sea, that the word could well describe the racecourse on any occasion.

The shape of the track, dictated by its position along the rim of the Downs, is unique among British racecourses: a straight six furlongs to which a triangular loop is attached by two bends (officially the Top and the Lower), one of which is used for some races, the other for others. Thus a race over one mile starts on the right-hand side of the triangular loop and joins the home straight by means of the Lower Bend – that is, the bend nearer the stands; a race over one mile one furlong starts near the top of the loop on the left and gets to the straight by means of the Lower Bend, whereas a race over ten furlongs starts at the same place but uses the Top Bend. Over a mile and a half, the race begins very near that start but goes round the top of the loop, using the Top Bend. Races over two and a half miles start near the stands, the runners going the reverse way up the straight before turning left up the Lower Bend, round the top of the loop, and returning to the straight by the Top Bend.

Confused? So, sometimes, are the poor souls who have to doll off the course to indicate to runners in each race where they should be going, and mistakes have been known to occur: the Festival Stakes won by Mtoto in May 1988 was declared void when it was discovered that the horses had been directed on to the Lower Bend rather than the Top, thereby cutting a considerable amount off their intended journey. It can also be confusing to jockeys: during the running of the Goodwood Cup a few years ago Greville Starkey on the leader helped his fellow riders by making elaborate hand-signals as the runners switched from the left-hand to the right-hand rail.

The course is undulating, especially in the straight, where the six-furlong course begins on such a stiff uphill rise that the stalls for that distance cannot be easily seen from the stands, whereas five-furlong races are run mostly downhill: Goodwood has a very fast course over the minimum distance. The luxuriant downland turf here provides one of the best racing surfaces in the country.

Apart from a jockey with a detailed course plan, what the ideal Goodwood horse most needs is a handy, fluent action, and the nimbleness and balance to cope with the undulating terrain. Relentless gallopers with a devouring stride need not apply.

The July Meeting, which takes place at the very end of that month – the week after the running of the King George VI and Queen Elizabeth Diamond Stakes at Ascot – and usually spills over into

August, is the high point of the Goodwood year, both in the quality
of the sport and in social cachet. If the emblem of Royal Ascot is the
top hat, at this meeting the panama comes into its own, and the
atmosphere is traditionally one of genteel relaxation. It was not
always so. Until 1906 morning dress was the order of the day at the
July Meeting, but that year Edward VII turned up wearing – horror
of horrors! – a lounge suit, giving as an excuse his opinion that
Goodwood was 'a garden party with racing tacked on'. Since then
the idea of Glorious Goodwood as a sort of garden party with a
purpose has persisted, though nowadays it has more of the atmosphere of a festival of quality racing.

The March Stand, opened by Her Majesty the Queen in 1980,
won the annual Concrete Society Award.

The high point of the five-day July Meeting comes on the
Wednesday with the running of the Sussex Stakes, a top-class event
over one mile (Lower Bend, please) which is Goodwood's only
Group One race. First run in 1841, the Sussex Stakes is one of the
top mile races of the year and always attracts a high-class turnout,
with winners since the war including the likes of Palestine, Petite
Etoile, Reform, Brigadier Gerard, Bolkonski, Wollow, Kris, On The
House, Chief Singer, Warning and Zilzal.

Frankie Dettori rode his first British winner at Goodwood: Lizzy Hare
on 9 June 1987. (The filly was named after trainer Luca Cumani's
secretary.)

Classy as it may be, the Sussex Stakes is rarely the medium for a
big gamble, and for punters (as opposed to purists) the high spot of
the July Meeting is the Stewards' Cup, a six-furlong handicap which
has long been one of the key betting heats of the whole season. The
sight of a thirty-strong Stewards' Cup field breasting the rise soon
after the start before hammering downhill towards the stands is one

of the most stirring in Flat racing: not quite so stirring, though as the sight of the horse you have been steadily backing for months going clear in the final furlong – a feeling familiar to supporters of 1988 winner Rotherfield Greys, who was backed from 40–1 to a starting price of 14–1 and reportedly won a million pounds for astute connections. Michael Tabor, owner of 1997 winner Danetime, admitted to winning 'a bit more than £200,000' on his horse. Other Stewards' Cup winners look gilt-edged in retrospect: the flying filly Lochsong won the race in 1992 carrying eight stone and starting at 10–1.

The other major races at the July Meeting include the Gordon Stakes over one and a half miles, a sound trial for the St Leger; the Richmond Stakes (six furlongs) for two-year-olds; the five-furlong King George Stakes, won twice by Lochsong; and the Nassau Stakes over ten furlongs for fillies of three years old and upwards, which usually produces a top-class field. The traditional centrepiece of the meeting is the Goodwood Cup over two miles, middle leg of the 'Stayers' Triple Crown' between Ascot and Doncaster.

Simon Holt's favourite . . .

'Goodwood is, I think, a very special place. A typically British course, with its tight turns and swinging undulations, it surely enjoys the most stunning setting of any racecourse in the world. Goodwood boasts lovely downland turf, good grand-stand facilities, a professional and innovative management team – and the standard of racing's not bad either.'

Goodwood's major meeting in the earlier part of the season comes in May, where the main interest is in the Predominate Stakes and Lupe Stakes, both over one mile and a quarter and trials respectively for the Derby and Oaks. Troy in 1979 was the last Derby winner to take the Predominate Stakes on the way to Epsom, but winners of the May race since then include 1988 St Leger hero Minster Son and, in 1995, Pentire, who was not entered in the Derby but won the 1996 King George VI and Queen Elizabeth Diamond Stakes. Height Of Fashion, dam of Nashwan, won the Lupe Stakes in 1982.

The August meeting features the Celebration Mile, first run in 1967 and boasting a roll of honour which includes Classic winners Humble Duty, Brigadier Gerard, Known Fact, To-Agori-Mou, Harayir and Mark Of Esteem.

On 30 July 1998 Double Trigger became the first horse ever to win the Goodwood Cup three times, following his victories in 1995 and 1997.

Goodwood's facilities are excellent. The stands are modern and well appointed, and if you don't like crowds you can still watch the racing from beyond the winning post on Trundle Hill, the venue where the less advantaged racegoing public traditionally went to watch the toffs promenading around in the Richmond Enclosure.

Racing was first staged at Goodwood, on the private estate belonging to the Duke of Richmond, in 1801, and the Goodwood Cup first run in May 1812. The main fixture switched to July in 1814, and for over a century and a half that was about all the racing that Goodwood offered each year. New autumn fixtures were introduced in 1965, and the May Meeting in 1968. From just four days' racing per year in the early 1960s, the course's annual programme now runs to around twenty.

It was at Goodwood in 1952 that public address was first used on a British racecourse.

Goodwood's reputation for innovation dates back to the nineteenth century and Lord George Bentinck, who established at the course several practices which in due course would become commonplace. Bentinck divided the viewing area into various enclosures (including one for cigar smokers!); reformed the method of starting races so that the starter used a flag, rather than (as was the practice before) simply shouting 'Go!'; introduced the notion of horses carrying numbers in the printed racecard; and established the pre-race parade ring and post-race unsaddling area.

Hamilton Park

Flat racing only, right-handed

Address Hamilton Park Racecourse Company Limited, Bothwell Road, Hamilton, Lanarkshire ML3 0DW
Telephone 01698 283806
Fax 01698 286621
E-mail hamilton@cqm.co.uk
Web www.jigsawelectronics.com/hamilton-park

Location Hamilton is 12 miles south-west of Glasgow; the racecourse is just north of the town between junctions 5 and 6 of the M74
Nearest station Hamilton West (from Glasgow Central): ³⁄₄ mile from course

Effect of the draw High numbers favoured in sprint races, especially when the going is heavy

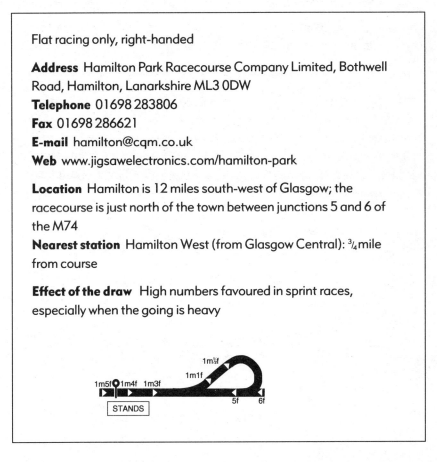

With marked undulations and a very stiff uphill finish, Hamilton Park puts the emphasis on stamina. The six-furlong course is dead straight, and all distances above six furlongs involve the right-handed pear-shaped loop attached to the straight course: fields for the longest distance run here, one mile five furlongs nine yards, start right in front of the stands then run 'the wrong way' away from the enclosures before veering left on to that loop. When the ground gets heavy here it can be very heavy, making the longer trips a real endurance test.

Since racing first took place in the area in the late eighteenth century, Hamilton has had a rather on–off sort of history – including a period when racing was discontinued for a while after only three horses arrived to compete at a two-day meeting in 1793! Racing was revived in 1800, then lapsed again for most of the nineteenth century, a new course opening in the Park in 1888, and folding in 1907. The current track was first used in 1926.

Hamilton Park was the first course in Great Britain in modern times to stage an evening race meeting – on 18 July 1947. The first race was at 6 p.m., and a crowd of 18,000 racegoers turned up. It was also the first course to stage a Saturday morning programme, on 8 May 1971 (thus avoiding competition with the Arsenal v. Liverpool Cup Final that afternoon).

Haydock Park

Flat and National Hunt, left-handed

Address Haydock Park Racecourse, Newton-le-Willows,
Merseyside WA12 0HQ
Telephone 01942 725963
Fax 01942 270879

Location Haydock Park is midway between Liverpool and
Manchester by the A49, less than a mile from the M6, junction 23
Nearest station Newton-le-Willows (2 miles from course);
Warrington Bank Quay and Wigan are each about 5 miles from the
course

Effect of the draw High numbers best in sprints, especially when
the going is soft

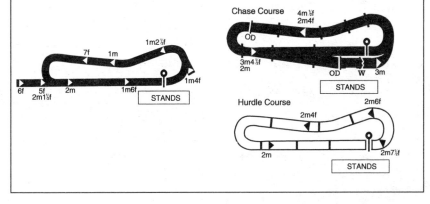

Haydock Park is without question one of the finest racecourses in
the country, with a high standard of racing under both Flat and
National Hunt codes, top-quality facilities for racegoers, and a track
which presents horses with a very fair test.

The circuit is a left-handed oval one mile five furlongs round, with
a right-hand dog-leg halfway down the back straight. There is a slight
rise up the home straight (which is nearly four and a half furlongs
long), but generally Haydock is flat with good bends, an ideal stage
for the galloping sort of horse. Races of five and six furlongs take

place on the straight course. For jump racing, the chase track is inside the Flat course, and the hurdles course inside that – which makes the hurdles circuit the shortest and sharpest of the three.

Red Rum's last race was at Haydock Park: starting at 33–1, he was unplaced in the Greenall Whitley Breweries Handicap Chase on 4 March 1978. In all he ran eighteen times at the course, winning twice.

Haydock Park stages a single Group One race on the Flat: the Sprint Cup, run over six furlongs in September. This race began life as the Vernons November Sprint Cup in 1966, and the first two runnings went to the great Be Friendly, owned by BBC commentator Peter O'Sullevan. Be Friendly was thwarted in his bid for a treble in 1968 when the race had to be abandoned on account of fog. In those days the Sprint Cup was run round a bend, but by the time the race attained Group One status in 1988 the course had installed the straight six furlongs. Since then the roll of honour has included such top-notch performers as Dowsing, Danehill, Sheikh Albadou and the finest sprinter of modern times in 1990 winner Dayjur.

Lester Piggott rode his first winner at Haydock Park – The Chase in the Wigan Lane Selling Handicap on 18 August 1948. He was twelve years old. Haydock was also the venue of Lester's last winner on British soil: Palacegate Jack on 5 October 1994. He was fifty-eight years old.

Other major Flat events include the Lancashire Oaks (July), the Old Newton Cup (also July), first run nearby in 1751, and the Rose of Lancaster Stakes (August), but it is as a jumping track that Haydock Park really excels. The fences are notably well built and some have a drop on the landing side, making the course an ideal place for Grand National preparations: in each of the five years that Red Rum ran in the Grand National his last outing before Liverpool was at Haydock.

Among the big jump races are the Tommy Whittle Chase over three miles in December (won by One Man in 1995 and The Grey Monk in 1997), the Peter Marsh Chase (three miles in January), Champion Hurdle Trial (two miles in January), Long Distance Hurdle (three miles in January), Greenalls Grand National Trial (three miles four and a half furlongs in February), and Swinton Handicap Hurdle (two miles in May).

The sport at Haydock is of a consistently high standard – there's never a dull day's racing here.

Hereford

National Hunt only, right-handed

Address Hereford Racecourse, Roman Road, Holmer, Hereford
HR4 9QU
Telephone 01432 273560
Fax 01432 352807

Location The racecourse is 1 mile north-west of the city on the A49
(Hereford–Leominster road)
Nearest station Hereford, 1 mile from course

Hereford is a right-handed, square-shaped track of about one and a
half miles round, with gentle undulations including a downhill run
towards the home straight. Its bends are mostly easy and thus it
favours the galloping horse, but many jockeys consider the fences
here to be stiff, and sound jumping can be at a premium, especially in
novice chases.

On 1 May 1975 there were so many runners at Hereford for what had
been planned as an evening meeting that several races had to be
divided. In the end the programme started at 1.30 p.m. and consisted
of fourteen races – the greatest number yet held on a single card in
Britain. Off-time of the last was 8.02 p.m.!

Racing at Hereford, which has been taking place in the great cathedral city since at least the late eighteenth century, tends to cater for the lower class of chaser or hurdler, but the course enjoys a strong local following and racegoers occasionally get the chance to glimpse a high-quality horse: 1982 Cheltenham Gold Cup winner Silver Buck, for example, won here twice in the 1979–80 season.

Hexham

National Hunt only, left-handed

Address Hexham Racecourse, High Yarridge, Hexham,
Northumberland NE46 2JP
Telephone 01434 606881
Fax 01434 605814
E-mail hexrace@aol.com

Location Hexham is about 20 miles west of Newcastle, and the
course is 2 miles south of the town; access from A69
Nearest station Hexham (Newcastle–Carlisle line), 1½ miles from
racecourse (free bus to course)

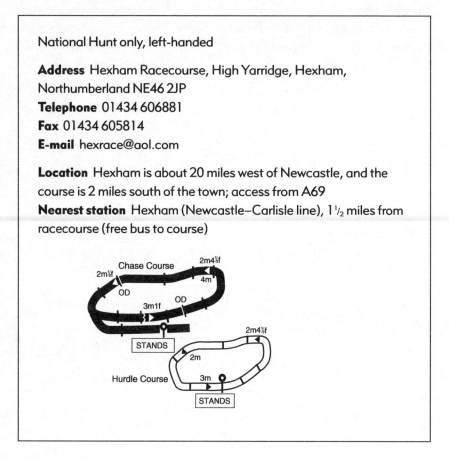

Set 800 feet above sea level and commanding glorious views across
the Northumbrian countryside, Hexham is one of the most scenic
courses in the country. In the eighteenth century races were held
down in Hexham itself, but the site in High Yarridge was established
late in the nineteenth, and those who make the steep climb from the
town are rewarded not only with stunning vistas, but with a course
whose homely rural charm and local feel are hard to match
anywhere.

Unsurprisingly, given its situation, the track itself – one and a half
miles round – is undulating, with a stiff climb out of the back
straight. In steeplechases, the finish is along a spur which bypasses

three fences in the straight. The fences are fairly easy but this is a testing track, with that climb to the home turn putting demands on a horse's stamina and resolution.

Bobby Renton, trainer of 1950 Grand National winner Freebooter and for a while of Red Rum, had his last ride in a race at Hexham when he was seventy-five years old.

Tommo's tip . . .
'Wrap up on a cold day! And concentrate on horses with plenty of staying power: that uphill finish really sorts them out.'

Huntingdon

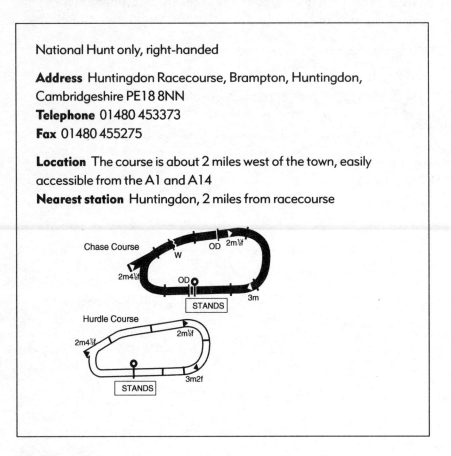

National Hunt only, right-handed

Address Huntingdon Racecourse, Brampton, Huntingdon,
Cambridgeshire PE18 8NN
Telephone 01480 453373
Fax 01480 455275

Location The course is about 2 miles west of the town, easily
accessible from the A1 and A14
Nearest station Huntingdon, 2 miles from racecourse

Huntingdon's circuit of one and a half miles round is flat and fast,
with easy bends and well-made fences – including an open ditch
right in front of the stands which provides one of the viewing
highlights here.

On 25 May 1998, Spring Bank Holiday Monday, Huntingdon staged
a race named after one of the area's most famous celebrities as part
of a programme in aid of the charity Mencap: the Norma Major
Maiden Hurdle.

Although not in the premier league of jumping tracks, Huntingdon hosts some very good races, notably the Peterborough Chase over two miles four and a half furlongs in November. This always attracts a small but high-class field: One Man, in his element at Huntingdon, saw off Viking Flagship in 1997, and previous winners include Sabin Du Loir (who beat Norton's Coin and Desert Orchid), Remittance Man, Martha's Son and Dublin Flyer. The Sidney Banks Novices' Hurdle, run in February, is a good pre-Cheltenham outing for staying novice hurdlers: 1998 winner French Holly duly went on to land the Royal & SunAlliance Hurdle at the Cheltenham Festival.

There has been racing on the present Huntingdon course since 1886, and the facilities are neat, compact and very well ordered.

Josh Gifford and his brother Macer were born in a farmhouse overlooking Huntingdon racecourse. Macer died in 1985, and is commemorated in a race here.

Kelso

National Hunt only, left-handed

Address Kelso Racecourse, Kelso, Roxburghshire TD5 7SX
Telephone 01668 281611
Fax 01668 281113

Location Kelso is 25 miles south-west of Berwick-upon-Tweed,
and the racecourse is 1 mile north of the town
Nearest station Berwick-upon-Tweed

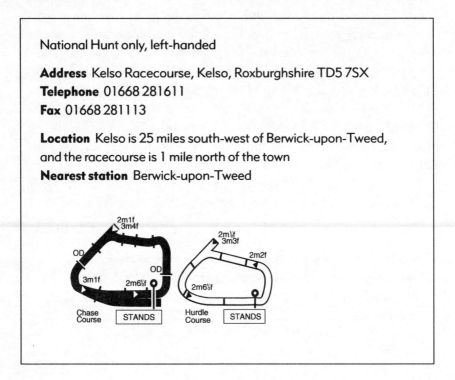

Set in the heart of the Border Country, Kelso is another of those
small rural jumping tracks which encapsulate the appeal of the
'gaffs'. The original grandstand, built by the fifth Duke of Roxburgh
when he established racing on this site in the early 1820s, is a
wonderful construction of stone and ironwork and still forms part
of the racecourse facilities, though it is now surrounded by a
higgledy-piggledy collection of more modern (and far less distinguished) buildings.

The hurdle course and the chase course diverge on the run away
from the stands, with the hurdle course cutting inside. Over hurdles
the circuit is about one and a quarter miles round and pretty sharp,
while the chase course is a furlong longer and puts a premium on
good jumping, as the fences here are well made and several are set on
the downhill stretch along the back. The run-in from the last fence,
on an elbow which avoids the two fences closest to the stands, is

uphill and over two furlongs long – a very tiring proposition for a horse trying to get home in heavy ground.

Kelso's best-endowed fixture is in early March, when an excellent card includes the final of the Hennessy Cognac Special Series for novice hurdlers – a race with £20,000 added prize money in 1998.

Tommo's tip ...

'Always pay serious attention here to horses trained by Mary Reveley or Gordon Richards.'

Kempton Park

Flat and National Hunt, right-handed

Address Kempton Park Racecourse, Staines Road East, Sunbury-on-Thames, Middlesex TW16 5AQ
Telephone 01932 782292
Fax 01932 782044
Web www.kempton.co.uk

Location Kempton Park is 1 mile north-east of Sunbury-on-Thames, half a mile from M3 junction 1; easy access from M25 junction 12

Nearest station Kempton Park (from London Waterloo), adjacent to course

Effect of the draw On the sprint course a high number is advantageous when the stalls are on the far side (especially in softer ground), a low number when the stalls are on the stands side

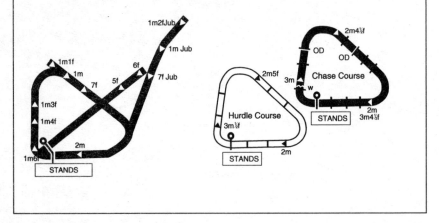

Kempton Park has undergone two major transformations since the early 1970s. First a new 'clubhouse', incorporating the weighing room, was built, and the old parade ring around which giants such as Arkle, Mill House and Mill Reef had walked was re-sited. Then the layout was revamped again in time for Boxing Day 1997. The inside of the grandstand was completely reordered, its crowning glory a glass-fronted panoramic restaurant along the lines of similar constructions at Wolverhampton and Cheltenham, and behind that grandstand was built a new parade ring, overlooked by the Philip Blacker statue of Desert Orchid.

During the Second World War the racecourse buildings at Kempton Park served as a camp for German prisoners of war.

Desert Orchid was completely in his element at Kempton Park, its level surface and tight right-handed turns suiting him like nowhere else: he won the King George VI Chase, Kempton's flagship event, no fewer than four times (1986, 1988, 1989 and 1990), and landed another three races here.

Kempton Park was opened in 1878, three years after the success of the park course experiment at nearby Sandown Park, and although it has never attracted the passionate devotion which Sandown regulars have for their stamping ground, it deserves its place among the major tracks of the land.

The circuit here is in the shape of a right-handed triangle, about one mile five furlongs round, intersected by a straight course for five-and six-furlong sprints, with the Jubilee Course – ten furlongs in length – forming a long spur which joins the round course just before the home turn three and a half furlongs out. The Jubilee course has slight undulations, but otherwise Kempton is flat.

Over jumps the course provides a very fair test, though speed and quick, accurate jumping are more important than sheer stamina: it is often thought, for instance, that a horse who could not get more than two and a half miles at Cheltenham would be able to stay the three-mile trip here.

Despite the generally high standard of racing, Kempton does not have a Group One race on the Flat: its best-known events on the level are handicaps – the two-mile Queen's Prize run at the Easter meeting (which also features two good three-year-old races in the Masaka Stakes and the Easter Stakes, both over one mile) and the Jubilee Handicap over one mile on May Bank Holiday Monday.

If the Flat racing programme is not out of the very top drawer, jumping at Kempton is right up there with the best. The three-mile King George VI Chase on Boxing Day is the most important weight-for-age staying chase of the season apart from the Cheltenham Gold Cup and has been won by most of the chasing greats – among them Arkle, Mill House, Mandarin (twice), The Dikler, Pendil (twice), Captain Christy (twice), Silver Buck (twice), Burrough Hill Lad, Wayward Lad (three times), The Fellow (twice) and, of course, four-times hero Dessie.

Arkle ran the last race of his career at Kempton Park: he was injured when second to Dormant in the King George VI Chase on 27 December 1966 and never ran again.

The Christmas meeting – one of the great racing occasions of the year, with a huge and hugely enthusiastic crowd – also has the Christmas Hurdle for the cream of the hurdlers: Lanzarote, Dawn Run and Kribensis (twice) all won this, and it was a fall from Night Nurse in this race in December 1977 which ended the career of the great jump jockey Paddy Broderick.

In February Kempton stages the Racing Post Chase, one of the very best handicap steeplechases of the year: Rough Quest won in 1996 and five weeks later landed the Grand National, while Desert Orchid's performance in winning under twelve stone three pounds in 1990 is widely considered the best of his distinguished career.

Kempton Park may not be the most scenic or the most glamorous racecourse in the country, but as the King George field is called into line on Boxing Day you wouldn't want to be anywhere else.

Leicester

Flat and National Hunt, right-handed

Address Leicester Racecourse, Leicester LE2 4AL
Telephone 0116 271 6515
Fax 0116 271 1746

Location The course is 2 miles south-east of the city centre on the A6, accessible from M1 junction 21
Nearest station Leicester, 2 miles from racecourse (bus to course)

Effect of the draw Middle to high numbers favoured on the straight course

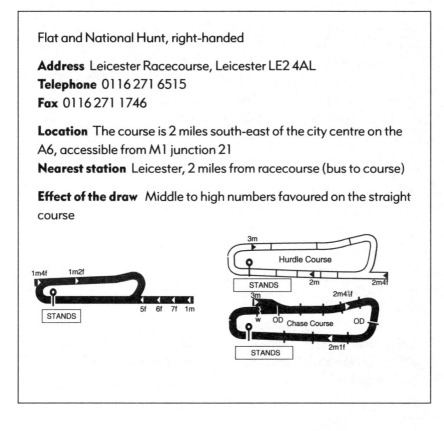

Leicester racecourse is a right-handed oval a mile and three-quarters round, with a run from the home turn of about four and a half furlongs; the straight mile is downhill until about halfway, with an uphill pull to the winning post, so the course needs a horse with a fair amount of stamina. A time to pay particular attention to Leicester is towards the end of the Flat season, when it often sees well-bred but late-developing two-year-olds from the top yards: for example, Sanglamore, winner of the Prix du Jockey-Club (French Derby) in 1990, had his first outing in a Leicester maiden race in November 1989.

The chase track runs inside the Flat course down the back straight, outside the Flat course in the straight; the fences are well made and the undulations – especially that uphill finish – make this a testing course for a jumper. The run-in from the last fence to the winning post is 250 yards.

Golden Miller, five times winner of the Cheltenham Gold Cup (1932–6) and the only horse ever to win the Gold Cup and Grand National in the same year (1934), scored his first victory at Leicester – in the Gopsall Maiden Hurdle (worth £83 to the winner) on 20 January 1931.

There has been racing at Leicester since the seventeenth century, and the present course at Oadby was founded in 1883. The Victorian grandstand built then was demolished and replaced in 1997 by a modern facility.

On 31 March 1921 a sixteen-year-old named Gordon Richards rode Gay Lord to win the Apprentices' Plate at Leicester – the first of the 4,870 winners which made Richards the most successful jockey in British racing history. Last of the six runners in that race was a horse named Toilet.

Lingfield Park

Flat (turf and all-weather) and National Hunt, left-handed

Address Lingfield Park Racecourse, Lingfield, Surrey RH7 6PQ
Telephone 01342 834800
Fax 01342 832833

Location Lingfield is 3 miles north of East Grinstead and the course is 1 mile south-east of the town on the B2028, about 8 miles north of the M25, junction 6
Nearest station Lingfield (½ mile from course)

Effect of the draw Low numbers mildly favoured in sprints on the all-weather course; on the turf course high numbers seem favoured

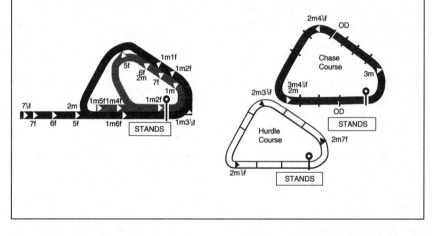

The image of 'Lovely Lingfield' took a knock when the laying down of the all-weather track turned the course's sylvan setting into a massive building site in 1989, and the existence of the Equitrack circuit inside the turf still takes the edge off the charm. Racing began here under National Hunt Rules in 1890, with the Flat following four years later, and it is as a Flat course that Lingfield is primarily significant today.

Left-handed and undulating, with a steep downhill run towards the final turn, Lingfield quite closely resembles the Derby course at Epsom Downs, and the Derby and Oaks Trials here, held in mid-

May and run over the full Classic distance of one and a half miles, are significant pointers to Epsom. Between 1983 and 1998 the Lingfield trials have produced four Derby winners (Teenoso, Slip Anchor, Kahyasi and High-Rise) as well as 1997 short-head runner-up Silver Patriarch, and in recent years the fillies' equivalent has likewise gone to three Epsom winners: Aliysa (who was subsequently disqualified), User Friendly and Lady Carla.

The first all-weather fixture in Britain was held at Lingfield Park on 30 October 1989.

The turf course is roughly in the shape of a triangle of a mile and a half round, with a run from the home turn of just under half a mile; races up to seven furlongs 140 yards run along a straight spur off the round course. Along the straight after the winning post the course rises to the top of the hill about six furlongs out, then descends sharply. The straight course is downhill for much of the way and considered an easy trip, and generally Lingfield is not a course which puts much premium on stamina: agility and nimbleness are more important here.

Rapporteur won nineteen races at Lingfield between 1989 and 1994, of which fourteen were on the all-weather surface.

The all-weather track is just under a mile and a quarter round, with no straight sprint course, and the shortness of the home straight – two furlongs – makes it imperative for a horse to be in contention turning in.

Plans to develop Lingfield as a training centre alongside its racing activities took a big step forward in July 1998 with the announcement that Gay Kelleway would become the course's first resident trainer. The long-term plan of the owner of the course, Arena Leisure, is to have as many as 350 horses in training there. But another development announced in July 1998 spelled the end of Lingfield jump racing, with the last meeting due to take place in March 1999.

Ludlow

National Hunt only, right-handed

Address Ludlow Racecourse, Bromfield, Ludlow, Shropshire
SY8 2BT
Telephone 01584 856221
Fax 01584 856217

Location The racecourse is about 2 miles north of the town, off the
A49 (Shrewsbury road)
Nearest station Ludlow (Newport–Shrewsbury line), 2 miles from
course

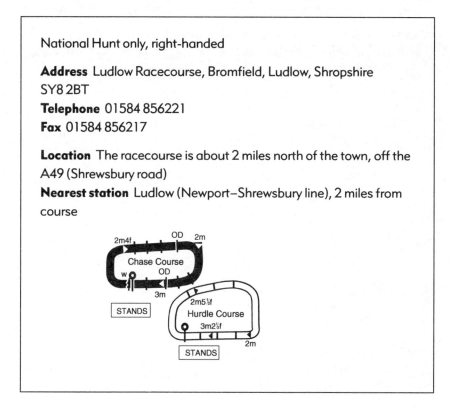

Ludlow boasts one of the quaintest buildings to be found on any
British racecourse, the open-topped grandstand built in 1904. That
is the good news. The bad news is that the track shares its land with a
golf course and has to tolerate no fewer than four road crossings,
which are covered by matting for racing but none the less serve as an
additional aggravation for jockeys trying to remember their way
round. For Ludlow is one of those tracks where the hurdle and chase
courses diverge down the back straight, and it is not unknown for
riders to take a wrong turning and incur the wrath of the stewards –
to say nothing of the punters.

The course has a few minor undulations but is generally flat. The
chase circuit, about one and a half miles round, has fairly tight turns
and is suited to the nippy sort of horse. Down the back straight the
chase course cuts across the golf course, while the back straight of

the hurdles circuit runs along the far side of the golf course and has easier turns than the chasing track.

Most racegoers visit Ludlow, an area where there has been racing since the eighteenth century, to experience its relaxed rural charm. Others claim to go there to consume the finest prawn curry to be had on any British racecourse. Whatever your reason, it's worth a trip.

Market Rasen

National Hunt only, right-handed

Address Market Rasen Racecourse, Legsby Road, Market Rasen, Lincolnshire LN8 3EA
Telephone 01673 843434
Fax 01673 844532

Location Market Rasen is 16 miles north-east of Lincoln; the course is on the eastern edge of the town on the A631; access from M18 junction 1
Nearest station Market Rasen, 1 mile from course

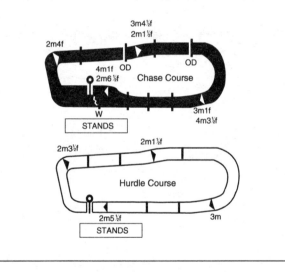

For the last few years Market Rasen has been the stage on which the curtain is rung down to end the jumping season, and in 1994 the course was the focus of racing attention as Richard Dunwoody and Adrian Maguire fought out the final round of their down-to-the-wire struggle for the jockeys' championship.

Even on less dramatic occasions, Market Rasen is an excellent course, for horse and human alike. The right-handed circuit is about ten furlongs round, with some undulations, and its comparatively easy fences render it a good testing ground for novice chasers. The turns are quite sharp, and the terrain tends to put the handy horse at an advantage over the big strong galloper.

The present course was first used in 1924, but most of the current facilities are much more recent: the two main stands, for example, were built in the 1960s. The water jump in front of the stands provides a good spectacle for the paying public, and overall this is a very racegoer-friendly course: the parade ring in front of the stands makes for ease of movement between paddock, betting ring, bar and stand; the facilities are kept as up-to-date as possible; viewing is excellent; and the highly popular summer evening meetings are graced with musical entertainment, underlining the notion that this is not a place to take racing too solemnly.

Tommo's tip ...

'I performed my first ever racecourse commentary here in 1967 and it always holds a special place in my heart.'

Musselburgh

Flat and National Hunt, right-handed

Address Musselburgh Racecourse, Linkfield Road, Musselburgh, East Lothian EH21 7RG
Telephone 0131 665 2859
Fax 0131 653 2083

Location Musselburgh is about 7 miles east of the centre of Edinburgh; accessible from Edinburgh ring road, A720
Nearest station Musselburgh East (from Edinburgh Waverley): bus from station; there is also a raceday bus from Edinburgh Waverley to the course

Effect of the draw Low numbers are favoured in 5-furlong races when the stalls are on the stands side, high numbers when stalls are on the far side

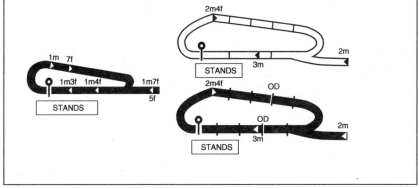

The racecourse formerly known as Edinburgh became Musselburgh on 1 January 1996, the new name more accurately reflecting the course's location, hard by the coast to the east of the city.

The circuit is a slightly undulating right-handed oval, about a mile and a quarter round, with sharp bends: the home turn is notoriously tight, but there is a run of about four furlongs before the winning post, so horses should have time to sort themselves out. Those bends conspire against the long-striding sort of horse, and Musselburgh is essentially a place for the handy type.

National Hunt racing has taken place here only since 1987. There are eight fences on the circuit (four on each straight), and the course favours front-runners.

A particular feature of Musselburgh is its climate. Being so close to the sea – which racegoers on the ground can sense, rather than actually see, beyond the back straight – the area enjoys temperate weather even when conditions are particularly wintry nearby.

Newbury

Flat and National Hunt, left-handed

Address Newbury Racecourse, Newbury, Berkshire RG14 7NZ
Telephone 01635 40015
Fax 01635 528354
E-mail newbury.races@pop3.highway.co.uk
Web www.sporting-life.com/racing/newbury

Location The racecourse is ¼ mile east of the centre of Newbury, 3 miles from M4 junction 13
Nearest station Newbury Racecourse (on the London Paddington–Swindon line), right by the entrance to the course

Effect of the draw No significant advantage

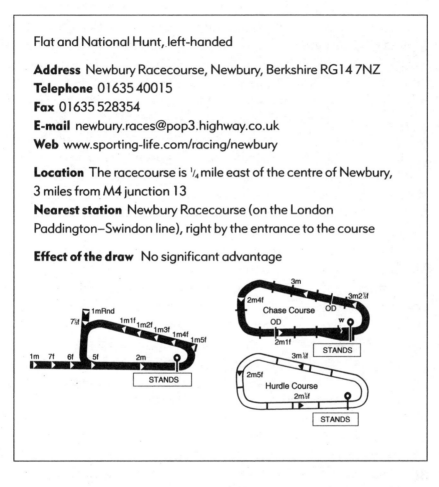

Talk about putting racecourses to different uses. Less than a decade after Newbury opened its gates to a crowd of 15,000 for the inaugural fixture on 26 September 1905, the First World War intruded. With racing here suspended during the hostilities, the course became a prisoner-of-war camp, then a hay dispersal centre, then a munitions inspection depot and finally a repair centre for tanks. Sport resumed in 1919, but twenty years later the country was at war again, and in 1942 the racecourse was taken over by the American forces as a supply depot. The turf – then as now one of the course's great glories – disappeared under a carpet of concrete and railway lines. In 1947 the course was released from war work, and racing resumed in 1949.

If horses could talk, they would doubtless voice their approval of Newbury, as few racecourses are more user-friendly than this. The ground is usually good or thereabouts, and the shape of the course is very well suited to a horse who likes to gallop, with a very wide track about a mile and seven furlongs round, sweeping, easy left-handed bends and no extreme undulations, though there are noticeable rises and falls in the straight. There is both a straight mile and a round mile on the Flat. Over the sticks the course is paradise for the long-striding type, but jumping ability is an important factor here as the fences are very stiffly built. There are five fences down the back straight, then the 'cross fence' before turning for home and five fences in the home straight, of which the water jump in front of the stands is omitted the final time round: runners veer right-handed round an elbow close to the winning post, and an experienced Newbury jockey can effectively cut off an encroaching rival here. Water jumps can cause horrible injuries to horses and are not too popular these days (many courses have dispensed with them), but if you've got it, flaunt it – and a large field of chasers streaming over the Newbury water jump is one of the great sights of racing.

The overall standard of racing at Newbury is very high, but it was not until 1995 that the course got its first Group One event on the Flat: the Lockinge Stakes on the straight mile, first run in 1958 (when it was won by the Queen's Pall Mall – whose portrait still graces the front page of every Newbury racecard). Since then the list of winners has included such illustrious names as Brigadier Gerard, Boldboy, Kris, Cormorant Wood (who dead-heated with Wassl) and Selkirk, and the quality of the race eventually led to its elevation to Group One. Soviet Line won the first two runnings of the race at that exalted level.

Newbury is an excellent trial ground for big races to come, and as the quintessence of a fair test is particularly popular with top trainers looking to give their two-year-olds a decent education. (The proximity of the course to Lambourn, the second great training centre in the land after Newmarket, underpins the quality of the horseflesh on view here.) Brigadier Gerard made his racecourse debut at Newbury – in the five-furlong Berkshire Stakes on 24 June 1970 –

and many years later his jockey Joe Mercer explained the course's attractions for juveniles: 'It's a very good place for a horse's first race. The ground is usually good, with an excellent covering of grass, and the track is wide open, giving the inexperienced horse plenty of room.' Other famous names which have graced the Newbury racecard as first-time-out juveniles – if only we'd known then what we know now! – are Shergar in 1980 and Lammtarra in 1994.

The course's top two-year-old races are the Mill Reef Stakes, run in September over six furlongs, and the Horris Hill Stakes, run over seven furlongs in October: notable winners of the latter include Supreme Court, Alcide, Charlottown, Kris, Kalaglow and Tirol.

During the building of the Berkshire Stand in 1992 a 'posterity box' was buried to afford future archaeologists of the site an insight into 1990s Newbury. The box contained a chamois leather used on the previous year's Derby winner Generous, a fine bottle of claret, and the day's editions of the *Sporting Life* and *Racing Post*.

Newbury also plays an important part in the early-season programmes of three-year-olds with aspirations, for whom the April meeting stages two seven-furlong events: the Greenham Stakes, a traditional trial for the colts' Classics (Wollow and Mill Reef both won this in the 1970s), and the Fred Darling Stakes, the equivalent trial for the One Thousand Guineas, which in the 1990s has been a springboard to Newmarket success for Salsabil, Shadayid and Bosra Sham.

Major Flat events at Newbury for older horses are the John Porter Stakes (one and a half miles in April), Geoffrey Freer Stakes (one mile five furlongs in August), Hungerford Stakes (seven furlongs in August) and St Simon Stakes (one and a half miles in October), while the September meeting now features an important trial for the Prix de l'Arc de Triomphe in the Doubleprint Arc Trial: Posidonas and Swain, first and third in the inaugural running in 1997, both went on to run at Longchamp.

Two races dominate the superb fare which Newbury stages for jump racing fans. The Hennessy Gold Cup, a handicap chase over three and a quarter miles at the end of November, moved to Newbury in 1960 after its first three runnings at Cheltenham and has long been one of the most eagerly awaited races of the National Hunt season: in terms of attendance and atmosphere, Hennessy day is Newbury's biggest and best fixture of the year. It's not hard to appreciate why: a large field of top-quality chasers hammering round almost two circuits of one of the best steeplechase tracks in the country – who could ask for anything more? The Hennessy has been won by many of the greats of modern times: Arkle (twice), Mill House, Mandarin (who won the race at both Cheltenham and Newbury), Stalbridge Colonist, Rondetto, Spanish Steps, Burrough Hill Lad and One Man. Another of the greats, Red Rum, was beaten a short head in the race in 1973.

If the Hennessy is the peak of the pre-Christmas phase at Newbury, the spring's highlight is the Tote Gold Trophy in February. Formerly the Schweppes Gold Trophy, this two-mile hurdle race is one of the big betting events of the year, with a lively ante-post market and (usually) a highly competitive field. The roll of honour bears such names as Persian War and Make A Stand – the only two horses to land the race and go on to win the Champion Hurdle the following month.

The Berkshire Stand at Newbury, opened in autumn 1992, replaced the old and much-loved grandstand and is now the centre-piece of Newbury's facilities. The hot dog served in the cavernous ground floor bar is best approached warily by those of a delicate constitution.

Newcastle

Flat and National Hunt, left-handed

Address Newcastle Racecourse, High Gosforth Park, Newcastle upon Tyne NE3 5HP
Telephone 0191 236 2020
Fax 0191 236 7761

Location The racecourse is 5 miles north of the city centre on the B1322, close to the junction of the A1 and A1056
Nearest station Newcastle Central, 4 miles from course

Effect of the draw On the straight course, horses drawn towards either rail seem to have an advantage; when the going is soft, low numbers are particularly favoured

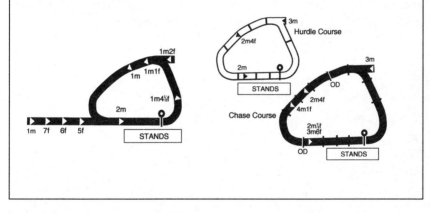

Newcastle is the home of the Northumberland Plate, still referred to as the 'Pitmen's Derby' and one of the major long-distance handicaps of the racing calendar. 'The Plate' – as it is known locally – was first run in 1833 and remains the highlight of the Flat at Newcastle, though the seven-furlong Beeswing Stakes, run in July, enjoys Group Three status: the race commemorates the famous nineteenth-century mare Beeswing, who won fifty-one races, including the Newcastle Cup six times.

Racing in Newcastle began on Killingworth Moor in the seventeenth century and moved to the Town Moor in 1721: the current

course at Gosforth Park was established in 1882. What greets the
present-day Newcastle racegoer is a course rapidly coming out of the
doldrums into which it had sunk a few years ago and now re-estab-
lishing itself as one of the top racecourses in the north.

The left-handed circuit is approximately triangular in shape and
one and three-quarter miles round; there is a straight course for
distances on the Flat of up to one mile. From the home turn to the
winning post is half a mile, with a steady climb to the finish putting
an emphasis on stamina. In general – and under both codes –
Newcastle is a course for the stayer, as the bends are gentle and the
galloping type of horse can really stretch out around here.

If the Northumberland Plate is the flagship event in the Newcastle
year on the Flat, the jumpers have their own big races. The Fighting
Fifth Hurdle (a limited handicap over two miles) in November is an
early-season opportunity for top hurdlers, while in February the
course stages a traditional Grand National trial in the Eider Chase
over four miles one furlong: the last winner of this race to go on and
win the National itself was Highland Wedding in 1969.

Newmarket

Flat racing only, right-handed

Address *(office)* Newmarket Racecourse, Westfield House, The Links, Newmarket, Suffolk CB8 0TG
Telephone 01638 663482 (*Rowley Mile course office* 01638 662762; *July Course office* 01638 662752)
Fax 01638 663044

Location Newmarket is 12 miles east of Cambridge; the July Course and Rowley Mile are both off the A1304; access from A45 and M11 junction 9
Nearest stations Newmarket station, 1 mile from the course by courtesy bus, has an infrequent service; Cambridge station, 12 miles from Newmarket, has a bus service to the course

Effect of the draw Little significant advantage on either course

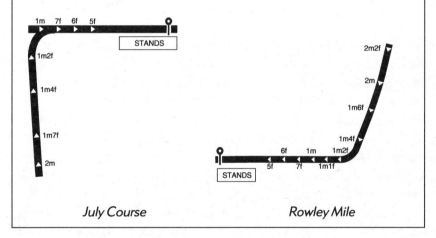

July Course   Rowley Mile

In the parlance of racing insiders, Newmarket is 'Headquarters' – largest training centre in the land and home of the Jockey Club, of the country's most prestigious bloodstock sales, of several famous studs (including the National Stud) and of two famous racecourses: the Rowley Mile, used for spring and autumn meetings, and the July Course for use during the summer.

The history of Newmarket as a centre of racing excellence goes back to the early seventeenth century and James I, a monarch who was devoted to hawking, hunting and riding despite his own physical drawbacks: according to turf historian Richard Onslow, James 'was slovenly, generally unwashed, and having a tongue too big for his mouth was constantly slobbering and dribbling'. (Does that remind you of anyone on the Channel Four Racing team?) On a hunting trip in the vicinity of Newmarket, the King was struck by the excellence of the terrain for his favourite sports, and had a house built there to accommodate him on his regular visits. In 1622 two of his courtiers raced their horses in a match for £100, and Newmarket racing had begun in earnest.

Tradition has it that the Cesarewitch is a race which begins in Cambridgeshire and ends in Suffolk. In fact runners on the Rowley Mile do not enter Suffolk until they are pulling up after the winning post.

When James died in 1625 he was succeeded by his son Charles I, who maintained the family devotion to outdoor pursuits and was himself a fine rider. But Charles fell foul of the executioner in January 1649 and five years later racing at Newmarket came to a halt: the Heath was ploughed up to prevent its use for hunting. After the Restoration the new King, Charles II, soon had Newmarket alive again, and spent a great deal of his time hunting and coursing there. Charles had a hack named Old Rowley, and his courtiers came to use the name of the monarch himself – a name that lives on, of course, in the Rowley Mile. The King rode in races (he is the only reigning monarch to have won an official horse race, having landed the Plate at Newmarket in 1671 and 1674), and built himself a palace on the site where now stands the Rutland Arms. Salacious tradition insists that a tunnel led from the palace to a house across the street in which lodged Nell Gwyn.

The royal connection with Newmarket was maintained after the death of Charles II in 1685. James II had little time on the throne, but his successor William of Orange bred racehorses, and won a £500 match at Newmarket with a horse who bore the enchanting name of Stiff Dick.

After the founding of the Jockey Club in about 1750 Newmarket became the administrative centre of racing, and although its headquarters is now in Portman Square, London, the Club maintains an elegant presence in the Jockey Club Rooms on Newmarket High Street, next to the National Horseracing Museum, a treasure-house very well worth a visit.

The two Newmarket Classics were both first run in the early nineteenth century – the Two Thousand Guineas in 1809 and the One Thousand Guineas in 1814 – by which time Newmarket was indisputably the leading racing community in the country. Today there are nearly three thousand acres of training grounds around the town, with some fifty racing stables housing two thousand horses in training. To be in Newmarket early in the morning and watch as the various strings work on the famous training grounds of Warren Hill or The Limekilns is one of the greatest sights in the sport, and it is always a thrill to spot your favourite charges of the big trainers – Cecil, Stoute, Cumani, Brittain, Gosden, and so many more, not least the Godolphin operation – in their home context.

The Tattersalls sale ring near the centre of town is the home of the top bloodstock auctions, including the sale in October when the cream of British yearlings come under the hammer, and for the racing devotee the perfect Newmarket day consists of early-morning attendance on the gallops, an afternoon's racing at the Rowley Mile, and an evening session at Tattersalls.

During the Second World War the July Course was one of the few racetracks at which racing was allowed to continue: most of the Classics – including the Derby from 1940 to 1945 – were run here during that period.

Newmarket has two racecourses. They share a stretch of track for about a mile from the furthest point from the stands, mostly downhill, then divide into two separate straights. (Between these straights is the Devil's Dyke, an ancient earthwork which stretches for miles across the Heath and inside which are reputedly buried the remains of armies who had fought with and against Boadicea.)

Newmarket stages seven Group One races, more than any other course in Britain.

The **Rowley Mile Course**, venue of all Newmarket's Group One races except the July Cup, is two and a quarter miles long, with a right-handed bend after a mile. Thus every race here of ten furlongs is run on a completely straight track, a configuration unique in the major racing countries. The course is exceptionally wide and the final straight mostly flat until the descent into the Dip, after which it runs uphill for the last furlong to the winning post. The Rowley Mile provides an unparalleled test for the big, long-striding horse, provided that the horse does not get unbalanced on that final downhill run, where jockeyship is at a premium. (About a furlong from the winning post are one of the Rowley Mile's landmarks, the Bushes – now a scrawny shadow of their former selves.)

Nowhere in Flat racing is there a more searching test than the Rowley Mile, which is why the course is home to no fewer than six races of Group One status:

- the first two Classics of the season in the Two Thousand Guineas (for colts and fillies) and One Thousand Guineas (for fillies only), both over one mile;
- three major two-year-old races in the autumn: the Middle Park Stakes (six furlongs) for colts, the Cheveley Park Stakes (six furlongs) for fillies and the Dewhurst Stakes (seven furlongs) for colts and fillies;
- the Champion Stakes over one and a quarter miles, last of the great middle-distance races of the season for older horses in Britain and invariably a race of the highest class: winners since the war include Petite Etoile, Sir Ivor, Brigadier Gerard (twice), Time Charter, Pebbles, Triptych (twice), Indian Skimmer, Bosra Sham and Pilsudski.

The first fixture of the year on the Rowley Mile is the Craven Meeting in mid-April, the moment when the Flat season moves up a gear after a low-key start at Doncaster and lesser venues: feature races here are the Craven Stakes (Group Three, one mile) and Nell Gwyn Stakes (Group Three, seven furlongs), respectively trials for the Two Thousand and One Thousand Guineas. At the other end of the season, the first October meeting includes the Middle Park Stakes and Cheveley Park Stakes for top two-year-olds, but the big betting vehicle is the Cambridgeshire, a handicap over one mile one furlong which provides one of the heftiest wagering events of the whole year.

Similarly, the second October meeting (formally known as the Houghton Meeting) provides sheer class in the Dewhurst and Champion Stakes, but the great punting moment comes with the Cesarewitch, a gruelling marathon over two and a quarter miles which in its time has been won by many of the great staying handicappers, such as Grey Of Falloden, John Cherry, Double Dutch and Vintage Crop, who was backed from 25–1 to 5–1 before winning by eight lengths in 1992.

An extensive programme of rebuilding over the last few years has greatly improved facilities for Rowley Mile patrons, a process which will be carried significantly further when the new grandstand is ready in 2000.

National Hunt racing at Newmarket – on a course the other side of the main road from the Rowley Mile – ceased in 1905.

On the **July Course** the run to the winning post from the right-handed turn is about two furlongs shorter than on the Rowley Mile, so that all races of up to a mile here are straight, along the course formally known as the Bunbury Mile, while longer races incorporate the bend. The longest distance run here is two miles. There are undulations for about the first three-quarters of the home straight, then the course runs downhill for about a furlong before a stiff uphill pull to the line – very similar to its companion course the other side of the Devil's Dyke.

As on the Rowley Mile, the ideal horse here is the long-striding type with no doubts about stamina.

The July Course stages what for many enthusiasts is the most relaxed of all the major fixtures on the Flat, the three-day July Meeting: panama hats get their first airing of the year; as the runners take their pre-parade ring constitutional in the cooling shade of a clump of tall trees, racegoers lean on the rail by the thatched weighing-room building (there's even a thatched Tote kiosk here); Pimms ranks top of the drinks list; owners and trainers congregate in the paddock around the creeper-bedecked gazebo.

Top of the bill at the July Meeting is the July Cup over six furlongs; the season's first Group One sprint race in Britain, it has been won by many of the great speedsters – including, in recent memory, such horses as Moorestyle, Marwell, Sharpo, Habibti, Royal Academy and Mr Brooks. The July Meeting also has the Princess of Wales's Stakes (one and a half miles), often a warm-up for the King George VI and Queen Elizabeth Diamond Stakes (Swain was second in 1997 en route to Ascot victory), and important two-year-old races over six furlongs in the Cherry Hinton Stakes for fillies and the July Stakes for colts and geldings.

These are the big events, but canny observers of any two-year-old maiden races here can pick up glowing hints for the future: Benny The Dip, Reams Of Verse and Cape Verdi, Classic winners in the last couple of years, all scored their first victories as juveniles in maiden races here.

If the key mood of the July Course is relaxation, this is nowhere felt more keenly than at the summer evening meetings which feature, after racing, a free pop concert. The acts may not always be in the first flush of their musical impact – Osibisa, The Searchers, The Hollies and Jools Holland were among the attractions in 1998 – but thousands of racegoers stay behind to listen and bop to the music long after the last runner has been washed down and boxed up for the homeward journey.

Newton Abbot

National Hunt only, left-handed

Address Newton Abbot Racecourse, Kingsteignton Road, Newton Abbot, Devon TQ12 3AF
Telephone 01626 353235
Fax 01626 336972

Location Newton Abbot is 16 miles south of Exeter; the racecourse is north of the town off the A380 (Exeter road); accessible from M5 junction 31
Nearest station Newton Abbot, ³/₄ mile from racecourse (bus to course)

Time was when Newton Abbot – where the present racecourse was established in 1880 – was the traditional curtain-raiser of the jumping season. Nowadays, with the summer jumping programme becoming embedded in the racing year, that honour lies elsewhere, but Newton Abbot's unpretentious fare remains a highly popular part of the jumping circuit in the West Country – especially with the holiday crowds who flock to the course for the summer fixtures.

The left-handed track is tight and flat, about nine furlongs round, with seven fences on the circuit and a noticeably short run-in from the last fence. Like so many of the small jumps tracks, Newton Abbot favours the speedy, nifty type of horse – which is just one reason why runners from the Somerset yard of Martin Pipe do so well here.

Nottingham

Flat racing only, left-handed

Address Nottingham Racecourse, Colwick Park, Nottingham
NG2 4BE
Telephone 0115 958 0620
Fax 0115 958 4515
Web www.demon.co.uk/racenews/nottingham

Location The racecourse is 2 miles east of the city off the B686;
access from M1 junctions 24 and 25
Nearest station Nottingham, 2 miles from course

Effect of the draw High numbers favoured in sprint races when
stalls on stands side, low numbers when stalls on far side

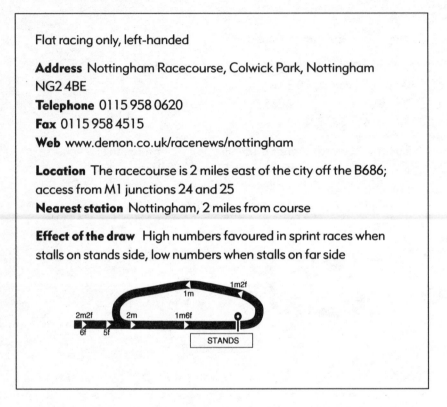

Despite objections from leading jumps trainers, National Hunt
racing at Nottingham finished after the 1995–6 season, and the
course is now used only for the Flat.

The circuit is a left-handed oval about a mile and a half round,
level down the back but with some minor undulations in the home
straight. Both bends are fairly tight, and the run from the home turn
to the winning post is four and a half furlongs. Races over five and
six furlongs are run on the straight course. Concentrate on the sharp,
well-balanced horse here.

Channel Four Racing's senior race commentator Graham Goode is a
director of Nottingham racecourse.

Graham Goode's favourite . . .

'Being involved with Nottingham has given me a greater appreciation of the many problems involved and the constant juggling, balancing and battles that have to be fought by every racecourse. But where else can you come racing, get a view of the paddock and all the action for as little as £2 a day?'

While not in the Premier League of British racecourses, Nottingham has the sort of terrain which often attracts young horses destined for great things: 1985 Derby winner Slip Anchor won here as a two-year-old, as did the great filly Oh So Sharp, who landed the 1985 One Thousand Guineas, Oaks and St Leger. Both horses were trained by Henry Cecil: you won't get a big price about a Cecil runner at Nottingham, but you will get a name for the notebook.

Lester Piggott's first retirement from the saddle came at Nottingham on 29 October 1985. That afternoon he rode Full Choke to win the Willington Handicap, his 4,349th winner in Britain. His 4,350th came nearly five years later – at Chepstow on 16 October 1990.

Racing has been documented in Nottingham since the seventeenth century, with the present course in use since 1892. A new grandstand was opened in 1992.

Perth

National Hunt only, right-handed

Address Perth Racecourse, Scone Palace Park, Perth, Perthshire
PH2 6BB
Telephone 01738 551597
Fax 01738 553021
E-mail sam@perth-races.co.uk
Web www.perth-races.co.uk

Location The racecourse is 4 miles north of the town on the
Blairgowrie road
Nearest station Perth, 2 miles from course

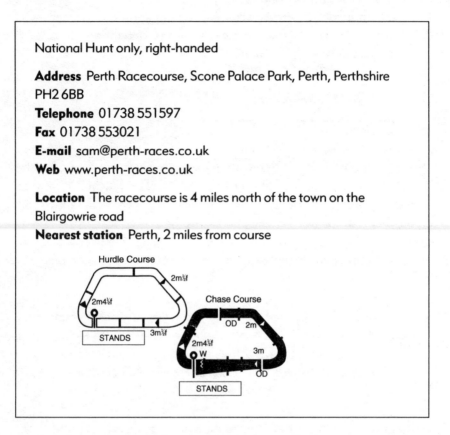

Perth racecourse – which opened in 1908, although there had been racing in the area in the eighteenth century – enjoys a glorious setting in the wooded parkland of Scone Palace, hard by the River Tay, and the river comes into its own when feeding the watering system which irrigates the course and thus makes possible its participation in the summer jumping programme.

Perth is the most northerly racecourse in Britain.

The track is a right-handed circuit of about a mile and a quarter round, the home straight longer than the back. It is mostly flat, with two tight turns and the other two much more gradual, and as a short circuit tends to favour the handy sort of horse. Front-runners can do well here.

Plumpton

National Hunt only, left-handed

Address Plumpton Racecourse, Plumpton Green, East Sussex
BN7 3AL
Telephone 01273 890383
Fax 01273 891557

Location Plumpton is about 10 miles north-east of Brighton; the
racecourse is 2 miles north of the B2116 (Lewes–Keymer road)
Nearest station Plumpton Green (London Victoria–Hastings line),
adjacent to the course

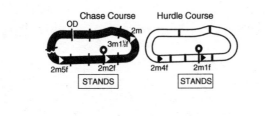

One of the most hair-raising sights in jump racing is a field of raw
novice chasers hammering at breakneck speed down the back
straight at Plumpton, a stretch of racecourse guaranteed to have any
sane racegoer sending thanks to heaven that the task of piloting
these horses is left to others. The runners take a fence as they enter
that back straight, then face a long and steeply downhill run to the
next, so that by the time they reach it they are usually going like bats
out of hell – with inevitable consequences for poor jumpers.

Manhattan Boy won fourteen races at Plumpton between 1986
and 1993.

At just nine furlongs round, with tight bends and those marked
undulations – the downhill rush of the back straight is balanced by

the uphill pull from the home turn – Plumpton is a course which much favours the handy, quick-jumping horse: the slower type, once adrift from the rest of the field, has little chance to make up ground here.

Like its neighbour Fontwell Park, Plumpton (where racing has been held since 1884) is very much a place for course specialists – human as well as equine.

Tommo's tip...

'Plumpton holds a unique place in my affections as I rode my one and only winner under Rules here, and the memories come flooding back every time I visit.'

Pontefract

Flat racing only, left-handed

Address Pontefract Racecourse, Park Lane, Pontefract, West Yorkshire WF8 1LE
Telephone 01977 702210
Fax 01977 600577

Location Pontefract is about 15 miles south-east of Leeds; the racecourse is in Pontefract Park, 1 mile north-west of the town, very close to the M62, junction 32
Nearest station Pontefract Tanshelf, close to the entrance to the park; Pontefract Monkhill is 1 mile from the course

Effect of the draw Low numbers favoured in sprint races

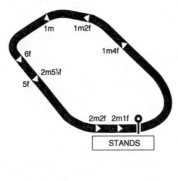

Racing at Pontefract dates back to at least the seventeenth century. During the Civil War, Cromwell's soldiers laid siege to Pontefract Castle, the last royalist stronghold, but despite this distraction the local race meeting went ahead, and over the succeeding centuries racing was a regular feature of local social activity. The present stands date back to 1919.

Stamina is the watchword at Pontefract, with its circuit of about two miles, marked gradients and long uphill run over the last three furlongs. There is no straight course, and the run from the sharp home bend is about two furlongs: in sprint races a horse needs to break smartly to avoid being cut off at that bend, so beware of slow starters here. Also, pay particular attention to jockeys with a good Pontefract record: this is a tricky course for horse and rider alike, and experience can be a crucial factor.

Pontefract is a good place to spot stars of the future running in comparatively humble surroundings. Silver Patriarch, short-head second in the 1997 Derby and winner of that year's St Leger, won a ten-furlong maiden race for two-year-olds here in October 1996, and 1998 Derby winner High-Rise opened his three-year-old campaign at the course.

Pontefract was a horseshoe-shaped track until the two ends were joined up in 1983 to form what is now the longest Flat racing circuit in the country. The distance of two miles five furlongs 122 yards is the second longest Flat trip in Britain (the longest being the two miles six furlongs of the Queen Alexandra Stakes at Royal Ascot).

During the Second World War, Pontefract was one of only two courses in the north where racing was allowed to continue (the other was Stockton). The Lincoln Handicap and Manchester November Handicap were run here during that period.

Tommo's tip ...
'Low numbers in sprints are always worth following..'

Redcar

Flat racing only, left-handed

Address Redcar Racecourse, Redcar, Cleveland TS10 2BY
Telephone 01642 484068
Fax 01642 488272

Location Redcar is 9 miles north-east of Middlesbrough; the
racecourse is in the town off the A1085
Nearest station Redcar Central, ½ mile from course

Effect of the draw Middle to high numbers seem to be a little
favoured on the straight course

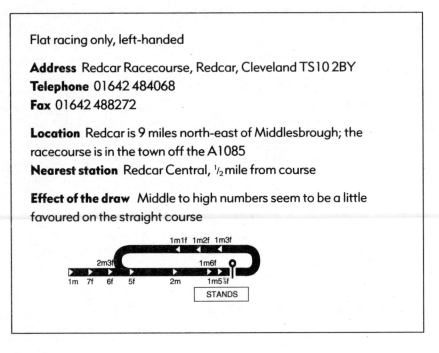

Two straights each six furlongs long, joined by two well-rounded
left-hand bends to make up a perfectly flat circuit of one mile five
furlongs, and a straight mile – Redcar offers an excellent course for
the galloping type of horse.

The present course was first used in 1871, before which racing
used to take place on the nearby sands. Under the direction of Leslie
Petch, an enterprising and influential clerk of the course, Redcar's
status grew steadily in the post-war years: for a while the Vaux Gold
Tankard, first run in 1959, was the most valuable handicap in
Europe. Today the course's main races are the Zetland Gold Cup, on
Spring Bank Holiday Monday, and the very valuable Two-Year-Old
Trophy run in October – worth over £69,000 to the winner in 1997.

Princess Anne – now the Princess Royal – rode her first winner on the
Flat at Redcar: Gulfland in the Mommessin Stakes on 5 August 1986.

Redcar can attract large crowds, especially on popular days such as Bank Holidays, but the stands are spacious enough to cope, and this is a very racegoer-friendly track.

Ripon

Flat racing only, right-handed

Address Ripon Racecourse, Boroughbridge Road, Ripon, North Yorkshire HG4 1UG
Telephone 01765 602156
Fax 01765 690018

Location Ripon is 10 miles north of Harrogate; the racecourse is south-east of the town on the B6265, with easy access from the A1
Nearest station Harrogate, 11 miles from course

Effect of the draw Low numbers appear favoured on the straight course

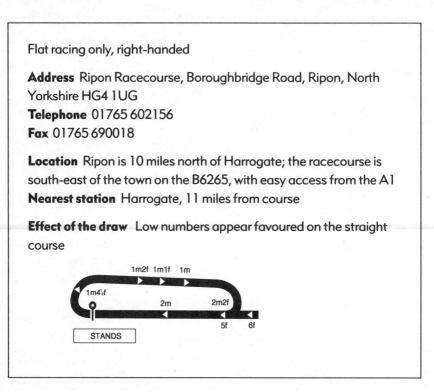

In shape and nature Ripon is reminiscent of Redcar (though the circuit here is right-handed) – long straights, sharp but well-rounded bends. The round course measures about thirteen furlongs, and the longest straight distance here is six furlongs, started from a spur. There is a dip a furlong from home and a few other minor undulations, making this a course on the sharp side.

Ripon has seen several racecourses since the sport was first recorded as taking place in the area in the mid-seventeenth century, and the first meeting at the present course took place in August 1900. Nowadays, with its catchment area encompassing the gentility of nearby Harrogate, Ripon has a very relaxed atmosphere – a mood reflected in the course facilities: lots of well-kept flower beds here.

Ripon's major race is the six-furlong Great St Wilfrid Handicap (named for the town's patron saint), run in August.

Salisbury

Flat racing only, right-handed

Address Salisbury Racecourse, Netherhampton, Salisbury, Wiltshire SP2 8PN
Telephone 01722 326461
Fax 01722 412710

Location The racecourse is 4 miles west of the city, just off the A3094 at Netherhampton
Nearest station Salisbury, 4 miles from the racecourse (bus to course)

Effect of the draw Low numbers tend to be favoured in sprints when the going is soft

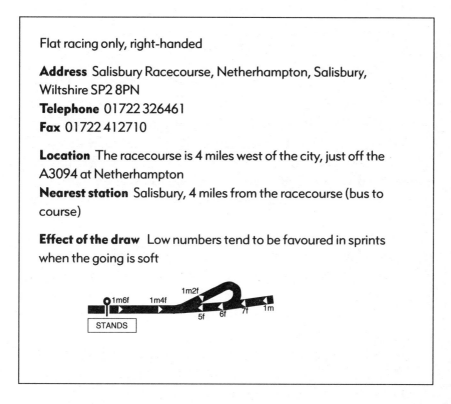

Queen Elizabeth I went racing at Salisbury in 1588 – supposedly on her way to see Sir Francis Drake just before his encounter with the Spanish Armada – and several of the all-time great horses have competed here, including Gimcrack, Eclipse and (somewhat more recently) Mill Reef. The Bibury Club, founded in 1681 at Burford in Oxfordshire and the oldest racing association in the world, moved to Salisbury in 1899 and established the present course, situated high on a hill above the town.

Steve Cauthen rode his first winner in Britain at Salisbury: Marquee Universal, trained by Barry Hills, in the Grand Foods Handicap on 7 April 1979.

Mill Reef, winner of the 1971 Derby, King George VI and Queen Elizabeth Stakes and Prix de l'Arc de Triomphe and one of the greatest horses of modern times, made his racing debut at Salisbury as a two-year-old on 13 May 1970. He won by four lengths at odds of 8–1, turning over 9–2 on favourite Fireside Chat.

The layout is similar to that of Hamilton Park: a straight (though in Salisbury's case that straight is decidedly dog-legged, with a right-handed elbow at about the five-furlong marker) to which is attached a right-handed loop. Races up to one mile use the straight; longer races take in the loop, so that the longest distance run here, one and three-quarter miles, is started in front of the stands, with the runners going away from the spectators before negotiating the loop and returning to the straight seven furlongs out. The first part of the loop is downhill, but most of the straight is decidedly uphill, and this is a very testing course.

Jim McGrath's favourite . . .

'Places like Cheltenham or York are invariably wonderful on account of the quality of the racing, but Salisbury has always held a special place in my affections, and I make sure I get there at least once a season. My first ever day as a Timeform racecourse reporter all on my own was at Salisbury in 1980, and I gave a large 'P' – the sign for a horse likely to show significant improvement – to a horse named Wicked Will, trained by Ian Balding for Paul Mellon. Next time out Wicked Will won at 10–1 – but I didn't back him! If you're going to Salisbury do your homework beforehand, and you could spot some stars of the future. In any event, it's never overcrowded, and there's no more pleasant place to spend a quiet afternoon's racing.'

Sandown Park

Flat and National Hunt, right-handed

Address Sandown Park Racecourse, Esher, Surrey KT10 9AJ
Telephone 01372 463072
Fax 01372 465205

Location Sandown Park is near the centre of Esher in Surrey, 4 miles
south-west of Kingston-upon-Thames; access from the A3 and
from M25 junction 10
Nearest station Esher (London Waterloo–Swindon line), on the far
side of the racecourse

Effect of the draw On the 5-furlong course, high numbers have an
advantage when the ground is soft and when the stalls are placed
on the far side; low numbers are favoured when the stalls are on the
stands side

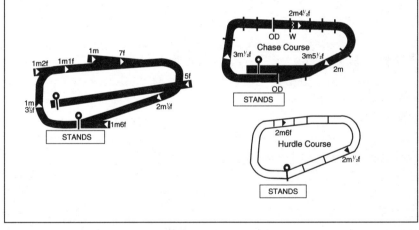

Sandown Park may not be the perfect racecourse – you can't get
sticky toffee pudding to die for, as you can at Carlisle, the view from
the stand is less spectacular than at Hexham, the atmosphere a shade
more serious than at Cartmel – but it is not far off.

The reasons for Sandown's huge popularity are not hard to find. It
is very accessible – on the edge of the metropolis and handy for the
M25. Viewing here is first-rate: writers may resort too readily to the

term 'natural amphitheatre' to describe the convenience of the stands' position on a rise overlooking the racecourse, but there is only a small and insignificant part of the round course where the runners are lost from sight, and the spectacle of a field of chasers attacking the fences in the back straight is one of the most uplifting in racing. The stand (divided into members' and grandstand enclosures: there is no silver ring here) is modern, having been opened in 1973, and facilities are good, with few bad bottlenecks for crowds on even the most populous days. But beyond those practical considerations, Sandown Park is an excellent place for spectators to come into close contact with the true heroes of the game, the horses, and this is most obviously felt as the runners walk to and from the course along the Rhododendron Walk, where racegoers can stand close to them without any barrier. Be they a collection of Derby aspirants before the Classic Trial or seasoned campaigners coming back in from the Whitbread Gold Cup, sweat-flecked, flanks heaving, snorting, nostrils aflare – and that's just the jockeys – being able to get so close is one of the great joys of the place.

Gordon Richards, most successful jockey in British racing history with 4,870 winners to his credit, rode the last race of his career at Sandown Park – third on Landau in the 1954 Eclipse Stakes. In the following race he was down to ride a filly named Abergeldie, owned (like Landau) by the Queen. But in the paddock before the race Abergeldie reared and fell on Richards, causing injuries which led to his retirement from the saddle.

The track itself is a right-handed oval about one mile five furlongs round, with the separate five-furlong course starting the far side of the home turn and having its own winning post a couple of hundred yards from the stands: the sprint course is quite straight, and rises steadily throughout. From the winning post on the round course the track climbs uphill into a fairly sharp right turn, then goes steeply downhill towards the back straight, which is level. At the far end of that straight the runners start to engage the very long, sweeping home turn which leads towards the entrance to the home straight about four furlongs out, and from there it is a steady uphill climb until the ground levels out shortly before the line.

The long straights and easy bends make Sandown a place for the galloping horse, and the steady incline up to the winning post – on both the round and the sprint courses – puts the emphasis on stamina. This is a testing course, and the horse must get the trip.

In 1947 Sandown Park became the first British racecourse to be covered live on network television.

Chasers here must be good jumpers, as the Sandown Park fences are very well constructed. There are eleven on the circuit, of which seven are in the back straight; the fence in the front of the stands is an open ditch on the near side, a plain fence (the last) on the far side.

The Henry II Stakes is named after the monarch who founded the Augustine priory which stood on the site in the Middle Ages. The pond which gives its name to the Pond Fence formed part of the priory grounds.

Take a two-mile chase as an example of the nature of the jumping course. The runners start near the entrance to the home straight and jump a plain fence and then the open ditch in front of the enclosures before climbing past the post and turning downhill. Acceleration on that downhill stretch makes the next fence especially trappy, but having survived that they swing into the back straight for those seven fences in a row – plain, plain, open ditch and water jump, then the Railway Fences, the key phase of any chase at Sandown: three plain fences, taken parallel to the railway line, set so close together that a horse must meet the first right to ensure a smooth passage over all three. The runners then negotiate the long right-handed curve before straightening out towards the Pond Fence, three from home. Get this right and you have the momentum for the final part of the race; get it wrong and you're struggling. After the Pond Fence the runners turn towards the second last, jump that, then take the last, a furlong from home, before knuckling down to tackle the desperately steep climb to the line. The complexion of so many chases at Sandown has changed as the horses hit that incline, and so often an apparently hopeless cause turns into victory. Chasers approach the winning line at Sandown at a different angle from hurdlers or runners on the Flat, which is why they have a separate winning post.

The hurdle course follows the line of the Flat track for most of the way, down the back straight switching from inside the chasing course to outside before passing the water jump. At the home turn it follows the Flat rather than the chasing circuit, and therefore the run from the last is not so steep as for the chasers.

A course of this quality merits a top-class programme, and Sandown Park patrons are rarely disappointed.

John Oaksey rode his first winner under Rules at Sandown Park: Pyrene in the Past and Present Hunters' Chase on 16 March 1956.

On the Flat, there is just one Group One event, but it's a cracker: the Eclipse Stakes, run over a mile and a quarter in early July. This is the first opportunity of the season for the cream of the three-year-old crop to take on the older generation at Group One level, and often the sparks fly. Since the war four current Derby winners – Tulyar, St Paddy, Mill Reef and Nashwan – have come to Sandown and successfully disposed of their elders to join a distinguished list of Eclipse winners which includes Ballymoss, Ragusa, Busted, Royal Palace (who won the Derby the year before his Eclipse), Brigadier Gerard, Ela-Mana-Mou, Sadler's Wells, Pebbles (first filly to win the race), Dancing Brave, Mtoto (the first dual winner this century) and Halling (also twice). Whatever the outcome, the relative merits of the generations are much more obvious after the running of the Eclipse Stakes, which makes it a pivotal event in the calendar.

Sandown's other big Flat races come in the spring. The Classic Trial over one and a quarter miles at the April meeting – on the same day as the Whitbread Gold Cup – has enjoyed a fine record in showing up horses who will run prominently in the Derby. Shirley

Heights was second in the race in 1978, and for the following three years the winner – Troy, Henbit, Shergar – went on to land the Derby; Shahrastani did likewise in 1986.

The meeting on Spring Bank Holiday Monday features the Temple Stakes over five furlongs and the Henry II Stakes over two miles, a good trial for the Ascot Gold Cup. The second day of the May meeting includes the Brigadier Gerard Stakes over a mile and a quarter, and the National Stakes for two-year-olds over five furlongs. In August, Sandown stages Variety Club Day, one of the big charity race days of the year.

The inaugural running of the Eclipse Stakes in 1886 was worth £10,000, more than double the prize money for that year's Derby. It was then the richest race ever run in Britain.

Sandown's principal jumping race is the Whitbread Gold Cup (three miles five furlongs) at the end of April – on a day which combines top-class jumping with top-class Flat racing (Classic Trial and Gordon Richards Stakes) to draw enormous crowds to the Esher track. The inaugural running of the Whitbread in 1957 was the first commercially sponsored horse race, and it has remained one of the top staying handicap chases of the year: its roll of honour includes Arkle, Mill House, The Dikler (who, ridden by Ron Barry, controversially got the 1974 race on the disqualification of Proud Tarquin and John Oaksey), Diamond Edge (one of three dual winners) and Desert Orchid. The 1984 running, in which the Queen Mother's Special Cargo beat Lettoch and Diamond Edge by a short head and the same, was described by John Oaksey as 'the most exciting steeplechase I have ever seen'. The Whitbread invariably presents a memorable spectacle, and represents the final high spot of the National Hunt season, then entering its twilight phase.

The quality of jump racing at Sandown Park is consistently high throughout the winter. An excellent card on a Saturday in early December has the two-mile Tingle Creek Chase, which commemorates the flying chaser whose spectacular jumping was seen to such effect at the course in the 1970s: he won the equivalent race three times, on each occasion setting a new course record.

Sandown jump meetings in the early months of the year give Cheltenham and Aintree hopefuls the chance to flex their muscles. January sees the Anthony Mildmay, Peter Cazalet Memorial Chase (three miles five and a half furlongs) which commemorates the famous amateur rider and legendary trainer who were two of the giants of National Hunt racing. February sees the Agfa Diamond Chase, a high-class handicap over three miles and half a furlong, and the Agfa Hurdle (two miles and half a furlong), a good Champion Hurdle trial. The Grand Military Meeting, with its centrepiece the Grand Military Gold Cup (a three mile and half a furlong chase for amateur riders), comes just before the Cheltenham Festival in March. Feature race on the second day of this meeting is the valuable Imperial Cup, a handicap hurdle over two miles and half a furlong which dates back to 1907. A large bonus has been put up for any horse who lands this and then wins at the Festival a few days later: most recent beneficiary was Martin Pipe-trained Blowing Wind, who netted an extra £50,000 for connections when landing the Imperial Cup and then the County Hurdle in 1998. (Olympian had won a similar bonus for the same stable when winning the Imperial Cup and the Coral Cup in 1993.)

Three Channel Four Racing presenters have ridden the winner of the Imperial Cup: John Oaksey on Flaming East in 1958, Brough Scott on Persian Empire in 1968, and John Francome on Prayukta in 1980.

The founding of Sandown Park, where the first meeting was run in 1875, represents a milestone in the history of British racegoing, for this was the first 'park' course, where the whole racecourse area was enclosed and everyone had to pay to get in (admission half a crown), rather than watch from common ground. One consequence of this was that the course could have more control over who came in, with the result that ladies could go racing without their sensibilities being assailed by foul-mouthed riff-raff: according to one early observer of this new phenomenon, Sandown Park was the only course 'where a

man could take his ladies without any fear of their hearing coarse
language or witnessing uncouth behaviour'.

Whether that holds true in the late 1990s is another matter
entirely. The air of gentility may have been displaced, but the quality
of the place – both of the course itself and of the sport it provides –
will ensure its enduring popularity.

In a song current at the time the course opened in 1875, a lady
gleefully anticipated 'a lark in the light or the dark – my silly old
man's at Sandown Park'. But silly her for not going with him.

John Oaksey's favourite . . .
'No surprises here! Sandown Park is simply the best steeplechase course in the world, both from the point of view of the
spectator and of the rider. I was always lucky there: my first
winner under Rules was at Sandown and I won the Imperial
Cup on Flaming East and the Whitbread on my beloved
Taxidermist. My only unhappy moment there was being
disqualified after winning the 1974 Whitbread on Proud
Tarquin after we'd beaten Ron Barry and The Dikler by a
head, but since I still know I did nothing wrong that day, it
doesn't hurt too much!'

Sedgefield

National Hunt only, left-handed

Address Sedgefield Racecourse, Sedgefield, Stockton-on-Tees,
Cleveland TS21 2HW
Telephone 01740 621925
Fax 01740 620663

Location Sedgefield is about 15 miles north-west of
Middlesbrough; the racecourse is 1 mile south-west of the town on
the A689; easy access from A1(M)
Nearest station Darlington, 9 miles from course

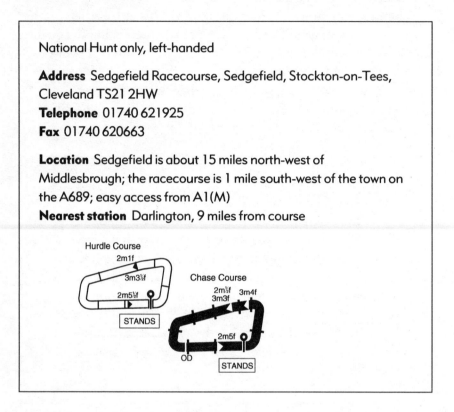

The town – or rather the constituency – of Sedgefield was sprung to
national prominence in May 1997 when the local MP, one Tony
Blair, became Prime Minister. Long before then the local racecourse
had been famous as the only British jumping track where the final
fence in a steeplechase was an open ditch, but that distinction was
removed a few years ago when the decision to do away with the
water jump in the straight provided the opportunity – readily taken –
to rearrange the configuration of fences and make the final obstacle,
as everywhere else, a plain fence.

Sedgefield's circuit is left-handed, about one and a quarter miles
round. It undulates markedly, and is essentially sharp – a track for
the handy horse. The run-in from the final fence is about 200 yards.

Organised racing at Sedgefield can be dated as far back as 1846,
with racing in the locality much earlier than that. Nowadays no one

would pretend that Sedgefield provides high-class racing, but its extremely strong base of local support makes it yet another of jumping's great 'gaffs'.

Southwell

Flat (all-weather) and National Hunt, left-handed

Address Southwell Racecourse, Rolleston, Newark,
Nottinghamshire NG25 0TS
Telephone 01636 814481
Fax 01636 812271

Location Southwell is 4 miles west of Newark-on-Trent and
14 miles north-east of Nottingham; the racecourse is 3 miles
south-east of the town at Rolleston; access from M1 junction 28,
then A38 to Mansfield and A617 towards Newark
Nearest station Rolleston, next to racecourse

Effect of the draw No advantage in straight 5 furlongs; low draw
favoured over 6 and 7 furlongs

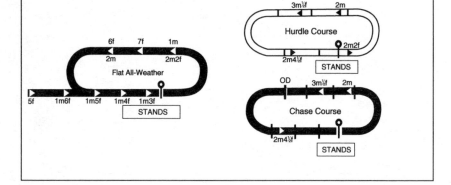

Until the advent of all-weather racing in 1989 there was little to be
said about Southwell. A very minor jumping track which had
opened in 1898, it provided modest sport for a mostly local clientele.

The acquisition of the course in the 1980s by Ron Muddle, who
had earlier brought a new lease of life to Lingfield Park, paved the
way for the installation of an all-weather track. Unlike at Lingfield,
where the all-weather track was fitted into the existing turf circuit, at
Southwell a completely new circuit was laid out and new facilities
built. It cannot be pretended that these stands and surroundings

dispense much in the way of atmosphere, but the course is very well appointed and well maintained, and no racegoer is going to have to wait long to be served at the bar here.

The all-weather track is laid out very much on the model of American circuits: left-handed, ten furlongs round and completely flat; five-furlong races start from a spur. From the home bend to the winning post is about three furlongs.

Tempering won twenty-two races on the all-weather at Southwell between December 1990 and March 1996. He won just one other race – on the turf at Redcar.

There is no turf racing on the Flat here, but jumping continues on turf on a course positioned inside the all-weather track, which makes it rather remote from the spectators. It is very sharp, though the fences here are considered fairly easy.

Stratford-on-Avon

National Hunt only, left-handed

Address Stratford-on-Avon Racecourse, Luddington Road,
Stratford-on-Avon, Warwickshire CV37 9SE
Telephone 01789 267949
Fax 01789 415850

Location The racecourse is 1 mile south-west of the town centre,
off the A439 to Evesham
Nearest station Stratford-on-Avon, 1 mile from course

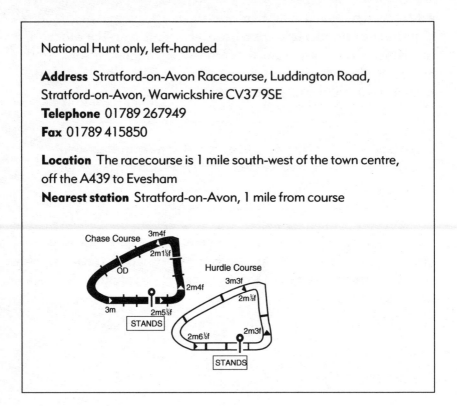

Highly popular with locals and with tourists who have temporarily
tired of brushing up their Shakespeare, Stratford racecourse is in the
shape of a left-handed triangle, one and a quarter miles round and
mostly flat, with tight bends which favour the handy horse over the
galloping type. The straight is about two furlongs long and the run-
in from the last fence under a furlong, so it is imperative for a horse
to be in contention at the final bend.

In 1967 the Horse and Hound Cup was won by Cham, ridden by
John Lawrence – now the Noble Lord himself, Lord Oaksey. They
won by one and a half lengths from Royal Phoebe, ridden by a
young amateur rider named Brough Scott.

Stratford has been the site of racing since the eighteenth century, and today the course stages sport of a fairly modest quality – though the Horse and Hound Cup, held on the last day of the season, retains its position as one of the year's most valuable and prestigious hunter-chases: its roll of honour includes the names of many of the great hunter-chasers, including triple winner Baulking Green (1962, 1963 and 1965) and quadruple winner Credit Call (1971, 1972, 1973 and 1975).

A new grandstand was opened in 1997.

Taunton

National Hunt only, right-handed

Address Taunton Racecourse, Orchard Portman, Taunton, Somerset TA3 7BL
Telephone 01823 337172
Fax 01823 325881

Location The racecourse is about 2 miles south of the town on the Honiton road, readily accessible from the M5, junction 25
Nearest station Taunton, 3 miles from course

With its notoriously tight bends, which until recent cambering work improved them could become very slippery in wet conditions, Taunton is not universally popular among jockeys. But as another of those staunchly unpretentious tracks catering to a strong and enthusiastic base of local support, it forms an integral part of the West Country jumping scene.

Taunton stages races over four miles two and a half furlongs, the longest distance in the calendar apart from the four and a half miles of the Grand National.

The right-handed circuit is sausage-shaped, with a run-in from the last fence of just 150 yards. The water jump is just beyond the stands, which denies spectators the full benefit of the spectacle which these obstacles are assumed to offer, but generally the viewing here is good.

National Hunt racing at the present course began in 1927, though there had been racing in the town of Taunton as early as 1802.

Tommo's tip . . .
'Martin Pipe's local track – enough said!'

Thirsk

Flat racing only, left-handed

Address Thirsk Racecourse, Station Road, Thirsk, North Yorkshire
YO7 1QL
Telephone 01845 522276
Fax 01845 525353

Location Thirsk is 24 miles north-west of York; the racecourse is on
the western side of the town on the A61 York–Ripon Road, with
easy access from the A1
Nearest station Thirsk, three-quarters of a mile from course

Effect of the draw Advantage for high numbers on the straight
course, more pronounced when the ground is fast

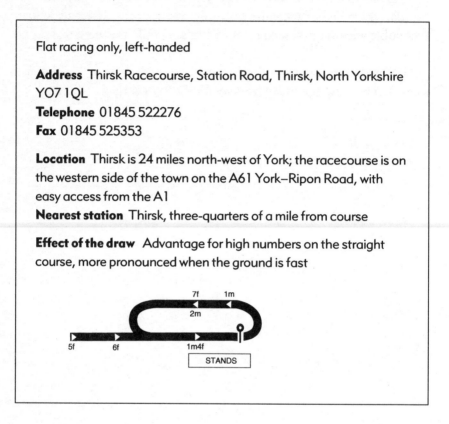

Racing has taken place at Thirsk since 1855, and although it may
not be one of the major Flat venues, it is such a good test of a young
racehorse that the course regularly forms the target of a raid from
one of the major trainers based in the south: runners from John
Dunlop's stable in Arundel, nearly 300 miles away, have a good
strike rate here, and most Thirsk racecards include a fair number of
runners from Newmarket, 185 miles distant.

The St Leger was transferred from Doncaster to Thirsk (and renamed
the Yorkshire St Leger) for the 1940 running on account of the war.

A left-handed oval a little over a mile and a quarter round, with minor undulations in the straight but otherwise pretty flat, Thirsk is on the sharp side but essentially a very fair course. Although its most valuable race is traditionally the Thirsk Hunt Cup run in May, the course also stages a significant Classic Trial at the April meeting: Tap On Wood won the equivalent race in 1979 en route to beating Kris and Young Generation in the Two Thousand Guineas.

Professional punter Paul Cooper took lucrative advantage of the effect of the Thirsk draw in the Dick Peacock Sprint Trophy over six furlongs on 20 May 1989. Aware that high numbers are favoured in sprints here, he permed high-drawn horses in Tricasts. There were twenty-three runners, and the result was:

1 Miss Daisy (drawn 21) at 20–1
2 Halvoya (drawn 23) at 25–1
3 Roysia Boy (drawn 22) at 33–1

The Tricast paid £13,673.17 to a £1 unit, and Cooper won around a quarter of a million pounds.

Towcester

National Hunt only, right-handed

Address Towcester Racecourse, London Road, Towcester,
Northamptonshire NN12 7HS
Telephone 01327 353414
Fax 01327 358534
Web www.demon.co.uk/racenews/towcester

Location Towcester is about 8 miles south of Northampton; the
racecourse is on the A5 south-east of the town
Nearest station Milton Keynes, 8 miles from course

Let's clear up one thing: it's pronounced 'Toaster' . . .

Located in the beautiful countryside of Lord Hesketh's Northamptonshire estate, Towcester is a course which gives the impression of space – a circuit of one and three-quarter miles round, good long straights, and a very easy bend out of the back towards the turn for home. A horse can really stretch out here, and the downhill run from the bend after the winning post is countered by a long hard slog out of the back, which taxes stamina to its limits. Towcester, especially in heavy ground, is no place for faint-hearted horses.

The present course was laid out in 1928 – though there was racing in the area in the last century – but the facilities have been constantly improved (a new grandstand was opened in 1997), the viewing is very good, and this remains an exceptionally pleasant venue for racegoing. It is also the ideal place to take a racing newcomer who wishes to get some flavour of the sport without the bustle of a bigger track.

It was at Towcester on 27 April 1989 that Peter Scudamore became the first jump jockey ever to ride 200 winners in a season.

Uttoxeter

National Hunt only, left-handed

Address Uttoxeter Racecourse, Wood Lane, Uttoxeter,
Staffordshire ST14 8BD
Telephone 01889 562561
Fax 01889 562786

Location Uttoxeter is halfway between Stoke-on-Trent and Derby;
the racecourse is on the south-eastern edge of the town, off the
B5017; access from M6 junction 14
Nearest station Uttoxeter (Derby–Stoke-on-Trent line), a short
walk from the course

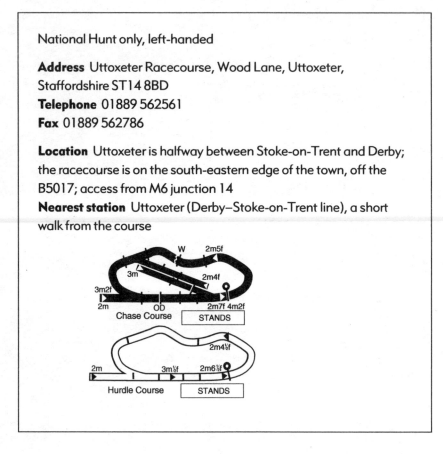

The circuit at Uttoxeter is about a mile and a quarter round, and to describe it as 'left-handed' is not telling the whole story, for the back straight of this popular Staffordshire course includes a marked right-hand kink – so that a horse on the inside in the early part of that stretch will find himself on the outside, only to regain the inner as the field tacks across to approach the home turn. Despite that unusual characteristic, this is essentially a galloping track, where the dour stayer can plug on resolutely – and in no event will his resolution be more needed than the Midlands Grand National, the major race of the Uttoxeter year. Usually held on the Saturday immediately following the Cheltenham National Hunt Festival in March, the

Midlands National is run over a distance of four and a quarter miles: a true slog, and any horse which performs well in this event must come into consideration for the Aintree marathon a couple of weeks later. The last Grand National winner to land the Midlands National was Rag Trade, who won the Uttoxeter race in 1975 and beat Red Rum at Liverpool the following year. The Thinker, winner of the 1987 Cheltenham Gold Cup, won the race in 1986. Lord Gyllene, winner of the 1997 National, had run second in the race in his outing before Aintree in the colours of Stan Clarke, whose enterprise had been so vital in reviving the fortunes of the track in the 1980s and 1990s.

Uttoxeter's other major race is the Classic Novices' Hurdle, run in November over two miles four and a half furlongs, which usually attracts a good-class field.

Racing took place in the area in the eighteenth century and has been held on the current course since 1907, but Uttoxeter today has a very modern feel. The Prince Edward Grandstand, symbol of the resurgence of the course's fortunes after many years as a jumping backwater, was opened in 1995.

Warwick

Flat and National Hunt, left-handed

Address Warwick Racecourse, Hampton Street, Warwick
CV34 6HN
Telephone 01926 491553
Fax 01926 403223

Location The racecourse is on the western edge of the town,
1 mile from junction 15 of the M40
Nearest station Warwick, ½ mile from racecourse (bus to course)

Effect of the draw Low numbers favoured in shorter races except
when the going is soft – in which case the stands side tends to run
faster

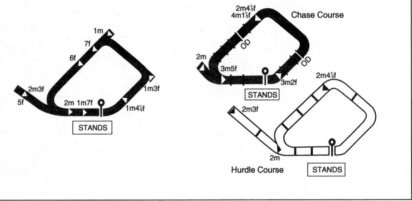

Racing at Warwick is first mentioned in 1714, and these days the
course is a popular venue under both codes.

The left-handed circuit is about one and three-quarter miles
round; five-furlong sprints start from a spur off the main course and
involve a left-hand dog-leg after about half the trip where the spur
joins the main course. With marked but not severe undulations,
Warwick is basically sharp in nature and puts the emphasis on speed
and agility rather than sheer galloping power.

The steeplechase track runs inside the Flat and has ten fences, five
of them in a good long run down the back straight.

Spectators' enjoyment is a little hampered by the runners disappearing from view for a while down the back, but the stands are a delightful mish-mash of the old and the new and patrons have every chance of seeing top horses on jumping days here – especially the pre-Cheltenham fixture in February when the card includes the Kingmaker Novices' Chase: Mulligan won that race in 1997 and Lake Kariba in 1998, when the same afternoon saw the final – and triumphant – racecourse appearance of the great chaser Dublin Flyer. The Crudwell Cup, in March, commemorates the last British racehorse to have won fifty races.

In May 1985 John Francome and Lester Piggott rode a match race at Warwick for charity. Lester on The Liquidator beat John on Shangoseer by three-quarters of a length.

Wetherby

National Hunt only, left-handed

Address Wetherby Racecourse, York Road, Wetherby,
West Yorkshire LS22 5EJ
Telephone 01937 582035
Fax 01937 580565

Location Wetherby is 12 miles north-east of Leeds and 12
miles west of York; the racecourse is east of the town just off
the B1224 road to York, very close to the A1
Nearest station Harrogate, 10 miles from course

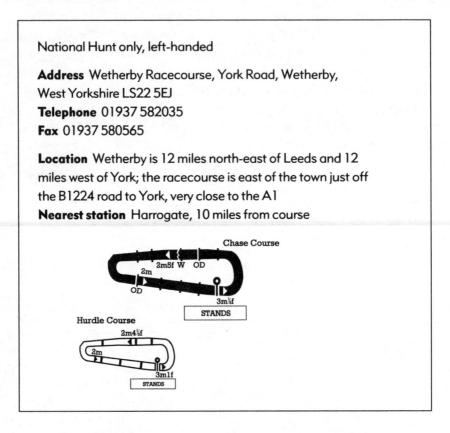

Things are changing at Wetherby. After years of complaint that the
facilities for racegoers there do not match the quality of the sport
which the course provides, there's a new weighing-room complex,
and the old stand is being replaced (completion is due by October
1999). From that stand spectators will enjoy a fine view of
Yorkshire's sole jumps-only track, a left-handed twelve-furlong oval
circuit with good long straights and little in the way of undulation.
The fences are very well built, and this is a course for the long-
striding, clean-jumping, galloping type of horse. It is no coincidence
that the late lamented One Man was in his element here, his three
course wins including back-to-back victories in 1996 and 1997 in
the Charlie Hall Memorial Chase – an important early-season event
for top-class three-mile chasers.

Wetherby's other major steeplechases are both run at the Christmas meeting: the Rowland Meyrick Handicap Chase (named after a famous former clerk of the course) over three miles one furlong on Boxing Day, and the Castleford Chase for two-milers the following day: winners of the Castleford Chase include such greats as Tingle Creek, Badsworth Boy, Pearlyman, Waterloo Boy (twice) and Viking Flagship. If those are the main races here, the overall standard of racing is high, with owners and trainers attracted by what is essentially a very fair course.

Racing was first held on the current track in 1891, though there had been jump meetings at a previous course in Wetherby, on the banks of the River Wharfe, since the 1840s.

Tommo's tip...

'One of my favourite jumping tracks. If they can win at Wetherby they can win anywhere.'

Wincanton

National Hunt only, right-handed

Address Wincanton Racecourse, Wincanton, Somerset BA9 8BJ
Telephone 01963 32344
Fax 01963 34668

Location Wincanton is 10 miles east of Shaftesbury; the racecourse is 1 mile north of the town on the A3081 (Shepton Mallet road); easy access from A303
Nearest station Gillingham (Dorset), 7 miles from course

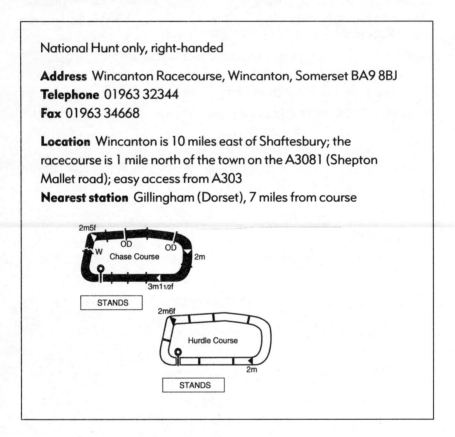

Wincanton – where racing has been held since the late nineteenth century – is a perennial favourite among West Country jumping enthusiasts and really comes into its own in the spring, staging several races guaranteed to provide serious pointers to the National Hunt Festival at Cheltenham in March. The Jim Ford Challenge Cup over three miles one and a half furlongs at the late February meeting is a traditional warm-up for the Gold Cup (Desert Orchid won the race in 1987), and at the same meeting the Kingwell Hurdle (two miles) provides a major Champion Hurdle trial; Dessie won this too, in 1984. Other classy Wincanton races include the Desert Orchid South-Western Pattern Chase (two miles five furlongs), run at the late October meeting, and generally the standard of sport here is high – significantly classier than at the other West Country courses of Newton Abbot, Exeter and Taunton.

Desert Orchid won six times at Wincanton: the Kingwell Hurdle in 1984, the Jim Ford Cup in 1987, the Terry Biddlecombe Chase in 1987 and 1988, the Silver Buck Handicap Chase in 1989 and the Racing in Wessex Chase in 1990.

From an equine point of view Wincanton is a very fair track – eleven furlongs round, right-handed, with easy bends and well-made fences, a good test both for the long-striding horse and the handier type. The undulations are not too severe, though the downhill run to the cross fence before the turn into the straight can find some jockeys going faster than they would ideally like.

Windsor

Flat and National Hunt, figure-of-eight

Address Windsor Racecourse, Windsor, Berkshire SL4 5JJ
Telephone 01753 865234
Fax 01753 830156

Location The racecourse is 1 mile north-west of the town on the A308 (Maidenhead road); close to M4, junction 6
Nearest stations Windsor & Eton Riverside or Windsor & Eton Central (bus – or riverboat – to course)

Effect of the draw High numbers favoured in sprints

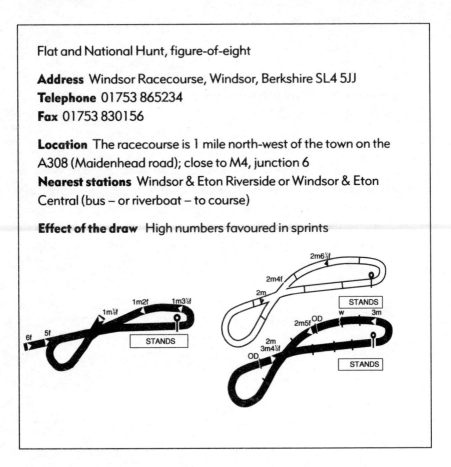

Windsor is a town oozing history, and it is no surprise that racing has been taking place here since at least the time of Henry VIII, with the present site used since 1866. A programme of evening fixtures was initiated in 1964, and nowadays the course is hugely popular with the crowds who swarm in on Monday evenings through the summer. Never mind the quality of the racing – this is the place for a jolly night out eating and drinking in the tree-filled enclosures, with perhaps the occasional glimpse of horse or jockey to remind revellers that they are at a sporting event. With a new grandstand opened in 1995, facilities for the 'ordinary' racegoer here are significantly better than they were a few years ago, though the viewing remains less than ideal. From 1999 there will in any case be less to view, as it was announced in July 1998 that jump racing at Windsor was to come to a halt at the end of the year.

Windsor bookmakers staged a strike in 1926 in protest against the imposition of a betting tax by Winston Churchill, then Chancellor of the Exchequer.

The course, about a mile and a half round the figure-of-eight, is quite flat, and at five furlongs the home straight is long enough to give a horse time to sort himself out after all those bends.

Windsor stages just one Group race, the Winter Hill Stakes (Group Three) over a mile and a quarter, run in August: Annus Mirabilis won the race in both 1996 and 1997.

Windsor was one of three southern racecourses allowed to carry on operating during the Second World War. The others were Newmarket and Salisbury.

Wolverhampton

Flat (all-weather) and National Hunt, left-handed

Address Wolverhampton Racecourse, Dunstall Park, Gorsebrook Road, Wolverhampton, West Midlands WV6 0PE
Telephone 01902 421421
Fax 01902 716626

Location The racecourse is 2 miles north of the centre of Wolverhampton off the A449 (Stafford road), with easy access from the M54, junction 2
Nearest station Wolverhampton (bus from station)
Effect of draw Low numbers favoured in sprints

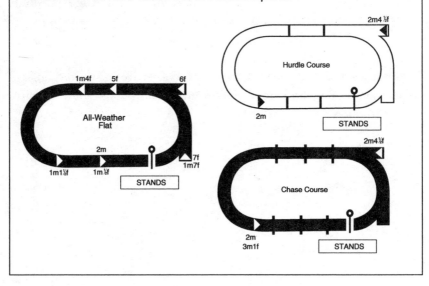

After serving as a low-grade dual-purpose track for over a century, Wolverhampton underwent a complete makeover in the early 1990s. The old stands and old circuit were discarded, and a new all-weather track was first used on 27 December 1993: that afternoon the course staged two races under floodlights, the first time horse racing in Britain had been illuminated. Wolverhampton was the somewhat unlikely venue for ushering British racecourses into a new era – a fact underlined by the £15.7 million development which went alongside the new track, including a 370-seat glass-fronted panoramic restaurant in the manner of American tracks. Purists complained that this was making a racecourse like a dog track, but the example was soon followed at Cheltenham and Kempton Park. On 29 May 1998 Wolverhampton, a byword for innovation in racing, unveiled a new design of starting stalls, prepared specifically for use at the track, which allow horses more room than the stalls in general use elsewhere.

Wolverhampton staged Britain's most valuable all-weather event in 1997: the Wulfrun Stakes, worth £31,086 to the winner. It is the only Listed race run on an artificial surface.

The all-weather circuit is extremely compact at just under a mile round, with no straight course. The bends are quite tight and the run from the home turn to the winning post just two furlongs, so the ability to lay up with the pace and be thereabouts turning in is of paramount importance here. The track is narrow in the home straight, and as a consequence a course rule dictates that the maximum number of runners in a Flat race at Wolverhampton is just thirteen.

National Hunt racing resumed at Wolverhampton, with two steeplechases on a new turf track on the outside of the all-weather, on 11 May 1997.

Tommo's tip ...
'An outstanding restaurant, from where you can watch all the action. Book early!'

Worcester

National Hunt only, left-handed

Address Worcester Racecourse, Pitchcroft, Worcester,
Worcestershire WR1 3EJ
Telephone 01905 25364
Fax 01905 617563

Location Worcester racecourse is close to the city centre, just off
the A449 (Kidderminster road); easy access from M5 junctions 6
and 7
Nearest station Worcester Foregate Street, 10 minutes' walk from
course

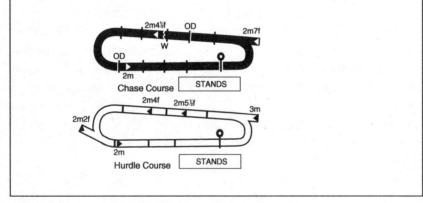

Worcester is an excellent place to spot the equine stars of the future,
as its long straights, easy bends and well-sited fences make it a good
course for novice chasers. For all runners, young or old, it provides a
fair test, and suits the strong galloper with plenty of stamina.

The left-handed circuit is one mile five furlongs round and very
flat; a particular hazard is that if a horse goes too wide at the home
turn he can end up in the adjacent River Severn: it has been known to
happen!

That river is the cause of Worcester's greatest problem – the
danger of flooding. The Severn has to rise only a little for the course
to become submerged, and waterlogging is a constant risk.

The current track was laid out in 1880, though there had been racing at this site long before then, and the course used to stage racing on the level: the last Flat meeting was on 20 August 1966.

The grandstand at Worcester, opened in 1975, was built at the wrong angle, so that runners disappear from view as they take the turn beyond the winning post. The mistake was not discovered until the stand was almost finished.

Yarmouth

Flat racing only, left-handed

Address Yarmouth Racecourse, Jellicoe Road, North Denes, Great
Yarmouth, Norfolk NR30 4AU
Telephone 01493 842527
Fax 01493 843254

Location The racecourse is 2 miles north of the town on the A149
Nearest station Great Yarmouth

Effect of the draw High numbers are slightly favoured on the
straight course

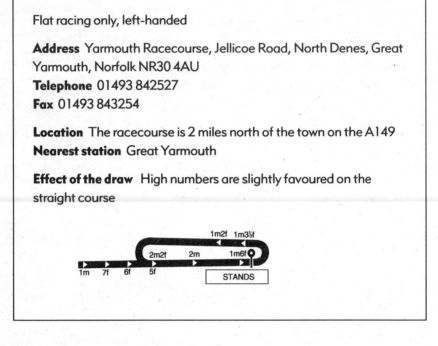

Yarmouth is the nearest Flat track to Newmarket, and trainers at
Headquarters who are not keen to expose their young horses too
soon to the yawning spaces of the Rowley Mile or the July Course
often bring promising two-year-olds here. So it can be a good place
for picking out embryo stars.

The track is a narrow left-handed oval about one and three-
quarter miles round, with distances from five furlongs to one mile
run up the straight, and apart from minor undulations the track is
flat. With its long straights, this is essentially a fair course, and
although the bends are quite sharp there is enough time up the home
straight to reach a decent position from which to mount a finish.
Thus it is a course for the long-striding, galloping type of horse. The
sandy soil drains quickly, so the going is rarely heavy.

The current track was established after the previous site, further
down the coast, was given over to redevelopment in 1920: there had
been racing on that spot since the early eighteenth century.

As with other seaside courses such as Redcar and Brighton, Yarmouth is very much a holidaymakers' course, and in the height of summer the atmosphere can get very boisterous.

York

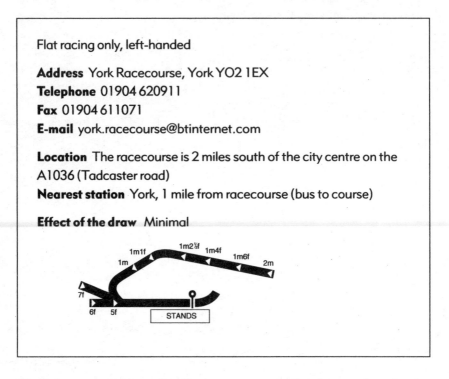

Flat racing only, left-handed

Address York Racecourse, York YO2 1EX
Telephone 01904 620911
Fax 01904 611071
E-mail york.racecourse@btinternet.com

Location The racecourse is 2 miles south of the city centre on the A1036 (Tadcaster road)
Nearest station York, 1 mile from racecourse (bus to course)

Effect of the draw Minimal

York has no rival as the finest racecourse in the north – in the opinion of many, no rival anywhere. For horses and spectators alike, it is superb.

Like the great city itself, racing here is wrapped in history. There were horse races at York in Roman times, when in AD 208 the ageing emperor Severus laid out a course on what is now known as the Knavesmire – the vast tract of common land just outside the city centre which later served, among other uses, as the site of common executions: three robbers were hanged there on the morning of 16 August 1731, and the same afternoon the first official race meeting took place on the Knavesmire. (A hint there for enterprising modern racecourse managements reeling in the crowds with non-racing activities?) The highwayman Dick Turpin was hanged here in 1739, again prior to the afternoon's sport.

In 1851 a crowd of over 100,000 watched the famous match between The Flying Dutchman and Voltigeur, each of whom had won a Derby and a St Leger. At five, The Flying Dutchman was a year older than his rival and had to concede eight and a half pounds in the two-mile race: he won by a length.

Today York shows due deference towards history – there is a very fine racing museum at the course which can be visited on race days – but in other respects is the model of a modern racecourse. The new grandstand, opened in 1996, has gone down very well with the public in the Tattersalls enclosure, while members in the County Stand likewise have very up-to-date facilities. Terraces afford excellent viewing of the unsaddling enclosure and the large parade ring, and the pre-parade takes place on a quiet, tree-lined lawn adjacent to the paddock. There is a sort of friendly grandeur to York which makes it a wonderful place to go racing.

The course itself is highly appreciated by jockeys and trainers, who consider it as fair a test of the Thoroughbred racehorse as there is – easy left-hand bends, wide track and long straights rendering it ideal for the long-striding galloper.

Although the Gimcrack Stakes is one of the course's best-known races, Gimcrack was beaten on both occasions he ran at York.

York's circuit is in the shape of a warped horseshoe, with two miles the longest distance on offer. Runners in a race of that distance start to the right of the stands and undertake a long gallop until making a gradual left-hand turn a little under ten furlongs from home: this takes them into a shorter straight which leads to the home turn, about four and a half furlongs out. There is a straight course for five- and six-furlong races, and seven-furlong races start on a separate spur, joining the straight by means of a very gentle dog-leg bend to the left. The course is completely flat.

Although the standard of racing at York is uniformly high, the three-day meeting in mid-August is its best fixture – and one of the very best of the whole Flat year.

Each of the three days has a Group One race.

Tuesday sees the International Stakes over a mile and a quarter, which links with the earlier Eclipse Stakes and later Champion Stakes as the three big ten-furlong races of the British Flat racing season. The International began life in 1972 as the Benson and Hedges Gold Cup and immediately made its mark, as Roberto's sensational three-length beating of the mighty Brigadier Gerard that year was the only defeat in the great horse's eighteen-race career. Dahlia won the race twice (beating Grundy in 1975), as did Ezzoud and Halling, and other top-notch winners of what is invariably a star-studded event include Troy, Commanche Run, Triptych and Singspiel.

Wednesday of the August Meeting has the Yorkshire Oaks, very often the next outing for horses who have won or run well in the Oaks or Irish Oaks, but above all Wednesday is Ebor day, when York stages its most famous race, the Ebor Handicap over one and three-quarter miles: this has been won by some very high-class performers, including the great Sea Pigeon, who lugged nine stone ten pounds (most of that weight being Jonjo O'Neill) to short-head victory in 1979.

The St Leger was run at York in 1945.

Thursday features the Nunthorpe Stakes, the only five-furlong Group One sprint of the year in Britain. Recent winners include Dayjur and Lochsong, but the most extraordinary running of this race came in 1997, when Kevin Darley on Coastal Bluff managed to run a dead-heat with Alex Greaves on Ya Malak despite his horse having lost his bit soon after the start: with no steering and nothing to hang on to except Coastal Bluff's mane, Darley rode a furious finish and just lasted home. For her part, Alex Greaves became the first woman to ride a Group One winner in Britain.

Other major races at the August Meeting include a serious St Leger trial in the Great Voltigeur Stakes (one and a half miles) and two races over six furlongs for two-year-olds: the Lowther Stakes for fillies and the Gimcrack Stakes for colts and geldings. To the owner of the winner of the Gimcrack goes the opportunity of sounding off with a speech at the Gimcrack Dinner in December.

York's other can't-miss meeting is in May, featuring important Classic trials over a mile and a quarter: the Dante Stakes is a major unraveller of clues for the Derby (recent winners of both races include Shirley Heights, Shahrastani, Reference Point, Erhaab and Benny The Dip) while the Musidora Stakes serves the same purpose in relation to the Oaks (winners of both include Diminuendo and Reams Of Verse). The Yorkshire Cup (one and three-quarter miles) at the May Meeting is an early-season outing for the top stayers.

Two other York fixtures which should be mentioned are the Timeform Charity Day in June, from which down the years over £2 million has been raised for various charities, and the Saturday in mid-July featuring what in 1998 was named the John Smith's Cup after over three decades as the Magnet Cup, first run in 1960 and supported by the oldest continuous sponsorship on the Flat.

John Francome's favourite . . .
'York: good facilities, great racing, wonderful atmosphere, nice people – and on a really good day you can smell the chocolate from the Terry's factory.'

Tommo's tours

Derek Thompson

One of the great joys of being able to go racing around the world with Channel Four Racing is the opportunity to experience different sorts of racetrack in all sorts of far-flung parts. While I wouldn't swap the great variety which the British tracks offer, when you travel round the racing globe the differences – and the similarities – are fascinating.

Let's start with **Ireland,** in so many ways the closest – in spirit and in the nature of the racing experience – to our domestic sport.

There are twenty-seven Irish racecourses, of which two – Down Royal and Downpatrick – are in Ulster. Remember that as far as racing is concerned there is no border: the Turf Club administers Irish racing, north and south.

Star turn among Irish racecourses is undoubtedly *The Curragh,* where all the Irish Classics are run (and shown on Channel Four), as well as many other major races. About an hour's drive out of Dublin in County Kildare, between the towns of Newbridge and Kildare, The Curragh is in many ways similar to Newmarket – a vast expanse of land serving as racecourse and as training centre for some 1,200 racehorses. Top trainers like Dermot Weld operate from here, and other familiar names such as Arthur Moore are not far away. Wide and very galloping in nature, The Curragh is a demanding track for horses: definitely no place for the doubtful stayer.

The only other Irish racecourse which stages Group One events on the Flat is *Leopardstown*. Set in suburban Dublin, Leopardstown is to many visiting British racegoers reminiscent of Sandown Park, though the circuit is left-handed while Sandown goes the other way. Top event on the Flat here is the Irish Champion Stakes in mid-September, always a great race (Pilsudski won it in 1997) and occasionally a gargantuan one: remember that amazing tussle between Dr Devious and St Jovite in 1992? Leopardstown also stages top-class sport over jumps, including the Irish Champion Hurdle (won by Istabraq in 1998 en route to his great victory in the Champion Hurdle at Cheltenham), the Ladbroke Hurdle (a highly competitive handicap) and the Hennessy Cognac Gold Cup, a valuable steeplechase run in early February and always a highly significant pointer to the Gold Cup at Cheltenham.

All great races, but Ireland's top steeplechase, the Irish Grand National, is run not at Leopardstown but at *Fairyhouse*, a short drive north-west of Dublin. We always cover the Irish National on Channel Four and it provides a great spectacle – not least when Desert Orchid landed the race in 1990, the only time he ever won outside Great Britain. Fairyhouse has good, modern facilities – which in all fairness can't be said of every Irish course. At *Laytown*, for example, up the coast from Dublin and the only place in Europe where official racing still takes place along the beach, the only permanent building is the gents' toilet! But racing at Laytown is an experience not to be missed if you're in the area: check carefully, though, as there's only one day's racing a year, and the time of the programme is dictated by when the tide is out.

Several Irish racecourses stage those great festival meetings which put such demands on the stamina and livers of racegoers. Perhaps the best known to Channel Four viewers is at *Punchestown* – not far from The Curragh – in April. The racing is top class and there's a strong British raiding party of horses fresh (though that's not always the right word) from Cheltenham and Aintree. David Nicholson is always keen to send a few over here: his Viking Flagship won on two of the three days in 1993, and in 1998 'The Duke' had some consolation for a blank Cheltenham Festival when Zafarabad won the big four-year-old hurdle. High point of the Festival is the La Touche Cup, run over four miles and a furlong across the unique bank course and taking in no fewer than thirty-one obstacles – the nearest the British Isles can offer to the Velka Pardubicka in the Czech Republic.

The Festival at *Galway* draws massive crowds to that great west-coast city. English-based jump jockeys – plenty of whom are Irish anyway – love to ride here, and stories of how the *craic* lasts long into the night are legion. Biggest races of the week are the Galway Hurdle and Galway Plate.

Among the other festival meetings are the six-day hooley at *Listowel* in County Kerry in late September. Nearby *Tralee* has its own big six-day meeting to coincide with the Rose of Tralee Festival in August. Gerry Crean, who runs the Green Man at Six Mile Bottom near Newmarket, very kindly took me along with Lester Piggott and some other friends a few years ago. The Crean family have run the racecourse for years and make everyone feel welcome: Irish hospitality here is legendary, and it's definitely worth a visit.

Further south in Kerry is *Killarney*, one of the most scenic courses in Europe, with lakes and mountains forming a glorious backdrop. The festival meeting here is in July. When Lester Piggott paid his first visit during his 'second career' in 1991 the reception he received was tumultuous, and he rewarded his fans by riding a treble for his old comrade-in-arms Vincent O'Brien. The Long Fellow was asked by the proud locals whether he'd ever ridden at a more scenic course. His reply: 'I've seen worse.' You can't say fairer than that!

Over in **France** there's no shortage of opportunities for *turfistes*, with over 260 racetracks scattered around the country. Many of these are provincial courses offering sport of a fairly modest nature, but a handful are major tracks familiar to Channel Four Racing viewers.

Principal among these is of course *Longchamp*. Situated in the leafy Bois de Boulogne very close to the centre of Paris, Longchamp has huge stands which can accommodate a hefty crowd. But it's really only on the first Sunday in October – the day of the running of the Prix de l'Arc de Triomphe, Europe's most prestigious race – that those stands are full, and on all but the biggest occasions racegoing in France can be a curiously tranquil experience. As well as the Arc and the Prix de l'Abbaye (the top-class five-furlong sprint run on Arc day), Longchamp stages three of the French Classics – the Poule d'Essai des Poulains (equivalent to our Two Thousand Guineas), Poule d'Essai des Pouliches (One Thousand Guineas) and Prix Royal-Oak (St Leger).

With its long downhill sweep towards home and its series of 'false straights' before the runners finally line up for home less than two furlongs out, Longchamp is a notoriously difficult course to ride, and punters do well to look for an experienced jockey here. To make matters even more complicated, there are two winning posts at Longchamp, and it is not unknown for an unfamiliar jockey to ride a finish to the wrong one!

The other two Classics in France are both run at *Chantilly*, the track about thirty miles north of the capital with one of the most dramatic backdrops of any racecourse in the world: Les Grands Ecuries ('the great stables'), part of a magnificent chateau built in the eighteenth century by the Prince de Condé, who was convinced that he would be reincarnated as a horse and wanted to have suitable accommodation ready!

Run a few days before the Derby at Epsom, the Prix du Jockey-Club is the French equivalent of the world's premier Classic, while the Prix de Diane is the French version of the Oaks (though it is run over a shorter distance than the Epsom race: one mile two and a half furlongs). For a while I worked in Chantilly as assistant trainer to Pierre Sanoner, and I once rode round the French Derby course: unlike our own Derby course at Epsom, it's pretty straightforward – flat, and with a good long right-handed bend into the straight.

The top race at *Saint-Cloud*, on the edge of Paris, is the Grand Prix de Saint-Cloud: the mighty Sea Bird II won this in 1965, Rheingold won it twice, and 1983 Derby winner Teenoso took the race on his way to the 1984 King George at Ascot.

In August all French racing roads lead to *Deauville*, the holiday town on the coast of Normandy. Highlight of a great week's racing here is the Prix Jacques le Marois over one mile, won in recent years by some of the top milers, including that superb filly Miesque, who landed the race in 1987 and 1988. But Deauville is about much more than just the racing. Major yearling sales take place here, and the town itself has the Casino and many wonderful bars and restaurants: no wonder it was always a favourite assignment for Big Mac when Channel Four was covering Deauville! The mood here is one of relaxation, but a very glamorous form of relaxation: when a few years ago I filmed a piece for Channel Four about the town, the head waiter at one of Deauville's top restaurants pointed out to me the tables reserved in years gone by for the likes of Prince Aly Khan and Elizabeth Taylor. More recently, the main patrons of that same restaurant have included one Cash Asmussen!

Comparisons between racecourses in Britain and **the USA** are so often drawn in favour of our domestic scene that you might think American courses are boringly monotonous. Not so. Admittedly the tracks themselves are all the same shape – left-handed ovals with regular bends – but the courses have different characters just like anywhere else.

The biggest race in the USA is the Kentucky Derby, run on the first Saturday of May at *Churchill Downs* in Louisville, Kentucky – the city whose most famous son is Muhammad Ali. Churchill Downs is instantly recognisable from the twin spires set on top of its grandstand, and on Kentucky Derby Day a crowd which can be counted in six figures pours into the stands and on to the infield inside the track, where all sorts of debauchery takes place. Traditional Derby Day drink is the mint julep, a concoction of bourbon, sugar, ice and mint so strong that if you have a couple before racing you're odds on to be flat on your back by post time of the big race! The great emotional moment at Churchill Downs is when the crowd sings 'My Old Kentucky Home' as the runners come out on to the track: they certainly know how to pull the heart strings in the States.

Churchill Downs is one of several North American tracks which have staged the Breeders' Cup, and it was a particular privilege for me to be there in November 1991 on the day when the François Boutin-trained phenomenon Arazi scorched home for that sensational five-length win in the Juvenile, undoubtedly one of the greatest individual performances in the history of our sport.

The Breeders' Cup is the nearest there is to a world championships of horse racing, and the courses which have staged this glittering occasion form a sort of premier league of North American tracks. In addition to Churchill Downs, for whom 1998 is the fourth hosting of the Cup (after 1988, 1991 and 1994), the courses are:

- *Aqueduct*, New York. It was here in 1985 that Pat Eddery and Pebbles landed the first British success in a Breeders' Cup race when taking the Turf.

- *Belmont Park*, New York – site of the famous 1990 Breeders' Cup which saw Dayjur and Willie Carson jumping the shadow in the Sprint, Royal Academy and Lester Piggott swooping late to land the Mile just days after Lester's return to the saddle, and the tragic death of Go For Wand. Belmont, which also staged the Cup in 1995 when the great Cigar won the Classic, is the home of the Belmont Stakes, third leg (after the Kentucky Derby and the Preakness Stakes at Pimlico, Baltimore) of the American Triple Crown.
- *Gulfstream Park*, Florida, which hosted the Breeders' Cup in 1989 and 1992, the year Lester had that terrible fall from Mr Brooks.
- *Hollywood Park*, California, hosted the inaugural Breeders' Cup in 1984, and welcomed it back in 1987 and 1997.
- *Santa Anita*, California. With palm trees swaying in the breeze, this is one of the most spectacularly beautiful courses in the world, and venue in 1986 for one of the most spectacularly disappointing performances by a British-trained horse in a Breeders' Cup race: Dancing Brave's defeat in the Turf. Santa Anita also hosted the Breeders' Cup in 1993.
- *Woodbine*, Toronto. In 1996 the Breeders' Cup moved outside the USA to Canada for the first time, to this well-appointed track in the suburbs of Toronto. It proved a memorable occasion, with Walter Swinburn marking his amazing recovery from his Hong Kong fall earlier that year with a sensational victory on Pilsudski in the Turf.

Greatest race of the year in **Australia** is the Melbourne Cup, run on the first Tuesday in November at *Flemington*, not far from the centre of Melbourne. It probably says something about the culture of Australian racing that its biggest event is a two-mile handicap, but I'm not sure what it is! The shape of the course at Flemington is reminiscent of Doncaster – left-handed, with a sweeping bend out of the back straight – but the atmosphere there on Melbourne Cup day is like nowhere else on earth, with everyone determined to enjoy themselves in their own individual ways, kitting themselves out in full morning dress, outrageous fancy dress or very few clothes at all. Plenty of tinnies are consumed but the mood remains one of huge enjoyment. The Melbourne Cup itself is a very tough race, and especially so for the British- or Irish-trained horses who, with huge improvements in equine air travel, are going over more regularly to challenge for one of the most prestigious prizes in world horse racing. For a horse to perform to his best after that long journey attests to a mighty constitution, and you have to salute the achievement of Vintage Crop in becoming the first ever horse from outside Australasia to win the race when storming home under Michael Kinane in 1993. Full marks to trainer Dermot Weld and owner Michael Smurfit for taking the bold step of sending their charge over from Dermot's stable in County Kildare: there's a statue of Vintage Crop at The Curragh, a fitting tribute to a truly great horse.

Flemington is also home to the Victoria Derby, run on the Saturday before the Melbourne Cup.

Two countries in the Far East are major centres of racing, and both generate such massive amounts of income through the level of betting that their racecourses offer top-class facilities.

Hong Kong has two tracks: *Happy Valley*, where racing has been taking place since 1846, and *Sha Tin*, built on reclaimed land and opened in 1978. Attendances at both courses reflect the gambling mania of the locals, and the atmosphere in the massive stands is one of fevered excitement. Many of our Flat jockeys go to ride in Hong Kong during the winter, and simulcasts of our big races such as the Grand National or Derby are beamed into the racetracks in the former colony.

In **Japan** the big race of the year, at least as far as the international dimension of the sport is concerned, is the Japan Cup run at *Fuchu* in Tokyo. This is an invitation race, and has been won by several familiar names from England or Ireland – including that hardy Irish mare Stanerra, Clive Brittain's tough-as-teak campaigner Jupiter Island, and Michael Stoute's great duo Singspiel and Pilsudski.

Fuchu regularly gets crowds of over 100,000 turning out for its Sunday fixtures, and they pack into a massive stand that runs practically the whole length of the home straight: this stand is three-quarters of a mile in length, nearly 100 feet high, and has five storeys with seating, balconies and restaurants. Sounds a bit different from Bangor-on-Dee!

Final stop on the tour – last but absolutely by no means least – is the oil-rich Gulf state of **Dubai**, where the Maktoum family have been so influential in making their tiny country a major player on the world racing stage.

How the family – and in particular the four brothers Sheikh Maktoum Al Maktoum, Sheikh Hamdan Al Maktoum, Sheikh Mohammed Al Maktoum and Sheikh Ahmed Al Maktoum – made themselves the main force in world horse racing has been well documented, as has the phenomenal success of Godolphin, the operation whereby the best of the Maktoum horses are conditioned in the warmth of the Dubai sun during the European winter and then returned to campaign in the top races: Cape Verdi's win in the 1998 One Thousand Guineas gave Godolphin the full set of the five English Classics, less than four years after their first with Balanchine in the 1994 Oaks – incredible!

For now I'm principally concerned with racecourses, and in *Nad Al Sheba*, the state-of-the-art facility just outside the city of Dubai which is now familiar around the racing globe as home of the Dubai World Cup, Dubai has one of the most important courses in the world.

With the first running of the Dubai World Cup in 1996 going to the great American horse Cigar, and the next two won by similarly famous horses in Singspiel and Silver Charm, the race has rapidly established itself. What of the course on which it is run? Nad Al Sheba, built on land on the edge of the desert a few miles outside Dubai and opened in 1992, is truly an up-to-the-minute track. Spectator facilities are superb – as will be agreed by the horde of English hacks who go over for the Dubai World Cup – and there's a pretty good course commentator there, though modesty forbids I should mention his name. Such has been the success of the venture that after only a couple of years the grandstand needed to be expanded – so the roof of the existing stand was removed, a new storey built, and the original roof put back. Talk about raising the roof!

The circuit is left-handed, about a mile and a quarter round and roughly triangular in shape, with a turf course running inside the dirt track. Alongside the racing, Nad Al Sheba is a busy training centre, and both tracks are used as gallops.

There is no betting allowed in Dubai, but for racegoers there is a free 'Pick 6': if you pick all six winners you can win a kilo of gold.

Dubai is a marvellous place to visit, not just for the racing but also to enjoy the sun, the sea, and the luxury hotels – one of which is rated seven-star!

Index

Page numbers in italic refer to the main entry on each course.